The Palgrave Kets de Vries Library

Manfred F. R. Kets de Vries, Distinguished Professor of Leadership and Development and Organizational Change at INSEAD, is one of the world's leading thinkers on leadership, coaching, and the application of clinical psychology to individual and organizational change.

Palgrave's professional business list operates at the interface between academic rigor and real-world implementation. Professor Kets de Vries' work exemplifies that perfect combination of intellectual depth and practical application and Palgrave is proud to bring almost a decade's worth of work together in the Palgrave Kets de Vries Library.

More information about this series at
http://www.palgrave.com/gp/series/16661

Manfred F. R. Kets de Vries
Leadership Unhinged

Essays on the Ugly, the Bad, and the Weird

Manfred F. R. Kets de Vries
INSEAD
Fontainebleau, France

ISSN 2730-7581   ISSN 2730-759X (electronic)
The Palgrave Kets de Vries Library
ISBN 978-3-030-79344-9   ISBN 978-3-030-79345-6 (eBook)
https://doi.org/10.1007/978-3-030-79345-6

© The Editor(s) (if applicable) and The Author(s), under exclusive licence to Springer Nature Switzerland AG 2021
This work is subject to copyright. All rights are solely and exclusively licensed by the Publisher, whether the whole or part of the material is concerned, specifically the rights of translation, reprinting, reuse of illustrations, recitation, broadcasting, reproduction on microfilms or in any other physical way, and transmission or information storage and retrieval, electronic adaptation, computer software, or by similar or dissimilar methodology now known or hereafter developed.
The use of general descriptive names, registered names, trademarks, service marks, etc. in this publication does not imply, even in the absence of a specific statement, that such names are exempt from the relevant protective laws and regulations and therefore free for general use.
The publisher, the authors and the editors are safe to assume that the advice and information in this book are believed to be true and accurate at the date of publication. Neither the publisher nor the authors or the editors give a warranty, expressed or implied, with respect to the material contained herein or for any errors or omissions that may have been made. The publisher remains neutral with regard to jurisdictional claims in published maps and institutional affiliations.

Cover credit: eStudioCalamar

This Palgrave Macmillan imprint is published by the registered company Springer Nature Switzerland AG.
The registered company address is: Gewerbestrasse 11, 6330 Cham, Switzerland

Contents

1 The Dark Cloud of Crowds   1

2 Let's Install Leaders for Life   15

3 The Little Drum Boy or the Rise and Fall of a Flawed Leader   35

4 A Strange Tale of Hatred   77

5 I Won't, Therefore I Am   101

6 Life Lessons from the "Great Mother"   119

7 When Lions Are Led by a Donkey   139

Index   143

About the Author

Manfred Florian Kets de Vries brings a different view to the much-studied subjects of leadership and the psychological dimensions of individual and organizational change. Bringing to bear his knowledge and experience of economics (Econ. Drs., University of Amsterdam), management (ITP, MBA, and DBA, Harvard Business School), and psychoanalysis (Membership Canadian Psychoanalytic Society, Paris Psychoanalytic Society, and the International Psychoanalytic Association), he explores the interface between management science, psychoanalysis, developmental psychology, evolutionary psychology, neuroscience, psychotherapy, executive coaching, and consulting. His specific areas of interest are leadership (the "bright" and "dark" side), entrepreneurship, career dynamics, talent management, family business, cross-cultural management, succession planning, organizational and individual stress, C-suite team building, executive coaching, organizational development, transformation management, and management consulting.

The Distinguished Clinical Professor of Leadership Development and Organizational Change at INSEAD, he is Program Director of INSEAD's top management program "The Challenge of Leadership: Creating Reflective Leaders," and the Founder of INSEAD's Executive Master Program in Change Management. As an educator, he has received INSEAD's distinguished teacher award six times. He has held professorships at McGill University, the École des Hautes Études Commerciales, Montreal; the European School for Management and Technology (ESMT), Berlin; and the Harvard Business School. He has lectured at management institutions around the world. *The Financial Times, Le Capital, Wirtschaftswoche,* and *The Economist* have rated Manfred Kets de Vries among the world's leading management thinkers and among the most influential contributors to leadership studies and human resource management.

Kets de Vries is the author, co-author, or editor of more than 50 books, including *The Neurotic Organization, Leaders, Fools and Impostors, Life and Death in the Executive Fast Lane, The Leadership Mystique, The Happiness Equation, Are Leaders Made or Are They Born? The Case of Alexander the Great, The New Russian Business Elite, Leadership by Terror, The Global Executive Leadership Inventory, The Leader on the Couch, Coach and Couch, The Family Business on the Couch, Sex, Money, Happiness, and Death: The Quest for Authenticity, Reflections on Leadership and Character, Reflections on Leadership and Career, Reflections on Organizations, The Coaching Kaleidoscope, The Hedgehog Effect: The Secrets of High Performance Teams, Mindful Leadership Coaching: Journeys into the Interior, You Will Meet a Tall Dark Stranger: Executive Coaching Challenges,* and *Telling Fairy Tales in the Boardroom: How to Make Sure Your Organization Lives Happily Ever After, Riding the Leadership Roller Coaster: A Psychological Observer's Guide, Down the Rabbit Hole of Leadership: Leadership Pathology of Everyday Life, Journeys into Coronavirus Land: Lessons from a Pandemic, The CEO Whisperer: Meditations on Leadership, Life, and Change,* and *Quo Vadis: The Existential Challenges of Leaders.*

In addition, Kets de Vries has published more than 400 academic papers as chapters in books and as articles (including digital). He has also written more than a hundred case studies, including seven that received the Best Case of the Year award. He is a regular writer for various magazines. Furthermore, his work has been featured in such publications as *The New York Times, The Wall Street Journal, The Los Angeles Times, Fortune, Business Week, The Economist, The Financial Times,* and *The Harvard Business Review*. His books and articles have been translated into more than 30 languages. He writes regular blogs (mini articles) for the *Harvard Business Review* and *INSEAD Knowledge*. He is a member of 17 editorial boards and is a Fellow of the Academy of Management. He is also a founding member of the International Society for the Psychoanalytic Study of Organizations (ISPSO), which has honored him as a lifetime member. Furthermore, Kets de Vries is the first non-US recipient of the International Leadership Association Lifetime Achievement Award for his contributions to leadership research and development (being considered one of the world's founding professionals in the development of leadership as a field and discipline). In addition, he received a Lifetime Achievement Award from Germany for his advancement of executive education. The American Psychological Association honored him with the "Harry and Miriam Levinson Award" for his contributions to Organizational Consultation. He is also the recipient of the "Freud Memorial Award" for his work to further the interface between management and psychoanalysis. In addition, he has also received the "Vision of Excellence Award" from the Harvard Institute of Coaching. Kets de Vries is the first beneficiary of INSEAD's Dominique Héau Award for "Inspiring Educational Excellence." In addition, he is the recipient of two honorary doctorates. The Dutch government has made him an Officer in the Order of Oranje Nassau.

Kets de Vries works as a consultant on organizational design/transformation and strategic human resource management for companies worldwide. As an educator and consultant, he has worked in more than 40 countries. In his role as a consultant, he is also the founder-chairman of the Kets de Vries Institute (KDVI), a boutique strategic leadership development consulting firm.

Kets de Vries was the first fly fisherman in Outer Mongolia (at the time, becoming the world record holder of the Siberian *Hucho taimen*). He is a member of New York's Explorers Club. In his spare time, he can be found in the rainforests or savannas of Central and Southern Africa, the Siberian taiga, the Ussuri Krai, Kamchatka, the Pamir and Altai Mountains, Arnhemland, or within the Arctic Circle.

management and psychoanalysis. In addition, he has also received the "Vision of Excellence Award" from the Harvard Institute of Coaching. Kets de Vries is the first beneficiary of INSEAD's Dominique Héau Award for "Inspiring Educational Excellence." In addition, he is the recipient of two honorary doctorates. The Dutch government has made him an Officer in the Order of Oranje Nassau.

Kets de Vries works as a consultant on organizational design/transformation and strategic human resource management for companies worldwide. As an educator and consultant, he has worked in more than 40 countries. In his role as a consultant, he is also the founder-chairman of the Kets de Vries Institute (KDVI), a boutique strategic leadership development consulting firm.

Kets de Vries was the first fly fisherman in Outer Mongolia (at the time, becoming the world record holder of the Siberian *Hucho taimen*). He is a member of New York's Explorers Club. In his spare time, he can be found in the rainforests or savannas of Central and Southern Africa, the Siberian taiga, the Ussuri Krai, Kamchatka, the Pamir and Altai Mountains, Arnhemland, or within the Arctic Circle.

Introduction

*Not everyone is capable of madness; and of those lucky enough
to be capable, not many have the courage for it.*
—August Strindberg

*When the world goes mad, one must accept madness as sanity;
since sanity is, in the last analysis, nothing but the madness
on which the whole world happens to agree.*
—George Bernard Shaw

The Dadaesque World We Live In

Looking at the world we live in, we cannot help but acknowledge the growing proliferation of populist, often demagogue-like, leaders, whose behavior is imbued with an almost surrealistic, Dadaesque quality. Many of these leaders seem to be engaged in a theater of the absurd, appealing to humankind's most basic instincts. However, such a theater of the absurd has the potential to become dangerous and can easily lead to disaster. And given what history has taught us, we cannot avoid or dismiss the warning signs. It is with all of this in mind and against the background of what I have learned about the darker side of these leaders' behavior that I undertook writing a number of essays, each of which grows out of the profound disquietness I have begun to feel about the world that's being created by them. This book offers a collection of these essays.

In this collection, not only do I discuss the psychological dynamics that facilitate the rise of populist, demagogue-like leaders, I also present a number of these essays in the form of fairy tales. Having written quite a few fairy tales over the years, I have learned that the use of this format can be quite illuminating.[1] Fairy tales have the capacity to stimulate the readers' creativity and imagination, and, in so doing, prove educational. But in particular, fairy tales provide the reader with moral guidelines. In that respect, fairy tales continue to play a significant role in our society, as they have in various societies for thousands of years. With the help of their kings and queens, heroes and villains, dragons and elves, fairy tales allow us to portray the various human dilemmas of leadership in a very stark tone. Often, these stories illustrate how leaders can be a force for the ugly, for the bad, and for the weird—as the title of this book suggests. In addition, I may at times resort to irony and metaphor as a way of making my point in the hope of prompting a better understanding of the darker side of leadership.

I strongly believe that leadership pertains to the ability to coalesce the efforts of many different individuals toward the achievement of common goals. Effective leaders are able to bring people together, make them better, and make them stronger. But to be able to do so implies that leaders need to set a moral tone. In fact, divorced from morality, leadership quickly becomes meaningless. And I would like to add that if leaders want to make a real impact, the values by which they govern should be transcendent—that is, those in a leadership position should grab the opportunity before them to make a real difference in society, to be a force for the good.

Furthermore, I also suggest that to be an effective leader necessitates that he or she is willing to undertake an inward-bound journey—an intense journey into the self. It's about acquiring a greater sense of self-awareness. It is all about self-improvement, about self-knowledge. After all, without self-knowledge leaders can easily be led astray. They may be tempted to act out their neuroses without consciously being aware of it. They may also become victims of hubris. It is for this reason that I will attempt to look not only at phenomena that appear on the surface, but also at what is happening under the surface. And to arrive at a greater understanding, I will resort to theories derived from psychoanalytic psychology (after all, in my other life, apart from being a professor of management, I am also a psychoanalyst), developmental psychology, neuroscience, and evolutionary psychology.

Unfortunately, with respect to the leadership equation, all too often, the Latin proverb "It is absurd that a man should rule others, who cannot rule himself" applies to too many of our contemporary leaders. Paradoxically,

---

[1] Manfred F. R. Kets de Vries (2016). *Telling Fairy Tales to the Boardroom; How to Make Sure Your Organization Lives Happily Ever After.* London: Palgrave Macmillan.

given their personality makeup, it often seems that people with the wrong kinds of motivations are drawn to search out a leadership role—people who aren't even capable of leading themselves.

Presently, the leaders that we need more than ever are people who also know how to unlock their followers' potential, who know how to help the people they lead to improve themselves. In fact, I would even go so far as to say that the ability to help their people grow and develop should be seen as one of the highest callings of leadership. After all, we rise by lifting others.

My hope is that these various essays will help the reader to better understand not only what's needed to be an effective leader but also to learn about the pitfalls of leadership—to recognize the warning signs when leaders transform into populist-like demagogues. I want the reader to become more aware of the psychological forces at work when groups of people resort to regressive practices. In addition, these essays will also speak to the importance of living a full life—and what gives our lives meaning. In this context, I will also make a few observations about the intricacies of male–female relationships given their importance, discussing in particular the feminine mystique. Consequently, I will address the question of what makes these relationships work.

I would like to conclude the introduction to this book by saying that effective leadership is not about making speeches or being liked. In many ways, leadership is about inspiring hope and defining reality. It is about the ability to unite people through the creation of meaning. And in my judgment, there is no more noble cause than to return people to the dignity of work and self-sufficiency, not to fall under the grip of arrogant ideologues and spineless detractors.

We want our leaders to do what's right, not what's easy. In fact, effective leadership is mostly defined by results—something that I view as being direly missing among many of the leaders that I am describing in these essays. Therefore, after everything has been said and done, what becomes apparent is that what we do has a far greater impact than what we say.

1

The Dark Cloud of Crowds

Those who can make you believe absurdities can make you commit atrocities.
—Voltaire

If you tell a lie big enough and keep repeating it, people will eventually come to believe it.
—Joseph Goebbels

Recently, once again, I saw *Triumph of the Will*, the infamous Nazi propaganda movie directed by Leni Riefenstahl, the famous German film director and Nazi sympathizer. The film remains well known for its striking visuals, showing some of the most enduring images of the leaders of the Nazi regime. It chronicles the 1934 Nazi Party Congress in the medieval city of Nuremberg, a town specifically chosen for this particular event to symbolize the link between Germany's Gothic past and its rising Nazi future. In the film, it is for all to see how Riefenstahl presents Hitler as the ultimate savior whose arrival on the scene would be the beginning of a supposedly "German Rebirth," bringing glory to the nation by creating an imagined Thousand-Year Reich.

In the early scenes of the film, we see how the Führer, like a contemporary god, descends from the sky in a plane. Subsequently, we find him surrounded by throngs of admirers, the camera capturing him through rows and rows of arms raised in the dreaded Nazi salute. And while Hitler is delivering his histrionic speeches, he is portrayed as a master conductor of a world of impeccably regimented subjects, who are lined up to create awe-inspiring human tableaus. Due to the intoxicating atmosphere created by these imposing crowds, every word spoken by Hitler is depicted as an inspired edict coming down from the heavens. And the filmmaker, in portraying these stark images—consciously or unconsciously—is showing how well she understood crowd psychology. She is demonstrating the kind of psychological dynamics that populist leaders know how to practice often in the most chilling of ways.[1]

The Siren Song of Populists

Sadly enough, given the way societies are developing, it has become increasingly clear that, in today's world, there are too many leaders who in their behavioral patterns display an alarming number of similarities to a terrifying individual like Hitler. They know how to take advantage of whatever a country's Zeitgeist may be as reflected in the mindset, attitudes, and values that have become mainstreamed. They know how to confront unequivocally the major anxieties of the populace in their time.

These populist-like leaders also know how to round up and excite people by demonizing other groups of people. To these individuals, xenophobia is par for the course. Unfortunately, while they are acting the way they do, too many of the people caught in their spell seem to be suffering from massive amnesia, forgetting the often-violent history that accompanies such leaders' stay in power. Given what these people are capable of doing, very disturbing behavior is to be expected. Writer and philosopher George Santayana pointed directly to the issue before us when he said: "Those who cannot remember the past are condemned to repeat it."

In encouraging their followers to do unimaginable things, some of these leaders have known no limits. In addition, what makes these people especially frightening is that many of them, in their desire to obtain power, are terribly seductive. Quite effectively, they turn into high priests of manipulation. They know how to cater to people's desire for magical thinking. All too often, however, by acting the way they do, these populist, demagogue-like leaders are comparable to "snake oil salesmen," merrily peddling their miracle cures, providing oversimplistic answers to difficult problems, while their solutions rarely are the correct ones.

---

[1] Gustav Le Bon (2009). *Psychology of Crowds*. London: Sparkling Books.

Populism

Generally speaking, the term populism applies to political movements that are situated outside the mainstream. It refers to a range of political stances that emphasize the idea that society is separated into two groups that are at odds with one another: the "pure" people versus the "evil, corrupt elite." This supposed elite consists of the political, economic, cultural, academic, and media establishments, which are portrayed as a homogeneous entity, accused of placing their own interests, and often the interests of other groups—such as large corporations, foreign countries, or immigrants—above what's important to the "pure" people. Naturally, it leads to the conclusion that these pure people have been seriously disadvantaged.

The popularity of these movements is very much due to general feelings of discomfort about the inability of liberal democracies to fulfill the promise of creating a better life for everybody. When that promise remains unfulfilled, the losers in this equation are tempted to search for some kind of "messiah" to defend themselves and their interests. They will be looking for someone able to stand up against the evil elite who, in their minds, have been unwilling to share their perceived advantages with others. It is a political approach that can have great appeal to the so-called ordinary people.

In addition, populist leaders, in seducing the masses, know how to take advantage of a primitive defense mechanism called "splitting," thereby creating an oversimplified world of "us" versus "them," of "good" against "evil," a way of looking at things that has no middle ground. Of course, while engaging in their demagogue-like activities, these leaders view themselves as being the representatives of the "good." At all times, they will reassure their audience that they have the interests of "the people" at heart, trying to defend them against this "evil elite" who are always portrayed as a corrupt and self-serving entity that has been taking advantage of the virtuous, hardworking population these populist leaders pretend to represent.

It is in this way that populist leaders manage to get their followers emotionally engaged by creating a binary *Weltanschauung* comprised of friends versus enemies. In fact, throughout history, the ability of *Homo sapiens* to create enemies—imaginary or otherwise—has always been a great way "to rally the troops," to create unity among a leader's followers. And this binary world consisting of "us" versus "them" becomes easier to latch on to when income stops growing or even starts to decline, when unemployment (especially among a country's youth) increases, and when poverty expands, bringing with it a growing income inequality.

Unfortunately, too often, in our day and age these societal developments have become a reality. No wonder that many people who have felt left behind are often plagued by anxiety and are angry. After all, income inequality is a perfect prescription for social unrest. It explains the attractiveness of these populist-like political or social movements that are challenging the entrenched values, rules, and institutions of democratic orthodoxy. But as I suggested before, these developments may be another instance of history once more repeating itself.

When reflecting back on various historical movements, the Spanish philosopher José Ortega y Gasset began studying the social upheavals in early twentieth-century Europe, which he saw as presenting a vision of Western culture that was sinking to its lowest common denominator while drifting toward chaos. In fact, many of the populist upsurges we are now witnessing worldwide can be interpreted—to use Ortega y Gasset's terminology—as a new "revolt of the masses."[2] And these rebellions are directed not so much toward the very essence of democratic forms of government, but rather as an uprising against an elite that appears to have failed to share their advantages with the common people. Of course, what's disturbing is that far too much of the world's economic gains have gone to the top 1% of the population.[3]

What needs to be added is that populist leaders—Donald Trump being a more recent, but very disturbing example—don't feel bound by institutional rules and regulations. Constitutional arrangements mean little to them. They strongly believe that the people whom they represent should be given the right to unbounded rule. No wonder, given their particular *Weltanschauung*, that they only pay lip service to frameworks for both enabling and restraining the exercise of public power. In reality, however, they aren't really interested in freedom of speech, assembly, an unallied judiciary, and an independent media. In fact, they're only interested in *their media*. These leaders are convinced that everything that they're doing is permitted, always pretending that they are speaking with the voice of what's conveniently described as "the silent majority." And to "rally the troops," they resort—as I have suggested earlier—to these primitive defense mechanisms such as splitting, often using minority groups as scapegoats to further their ends.

Unfortunately, all too often, much of their irresponsible behavior has been expedited by the social media. In their hands, rumors and lies easily become transformed into believable facts. And their rumors, by far, travel at a speed too fast to fall victim to fact checking. Thus, what has become increasingly

---

[2] Jose Ortega y Gasset (1994). *The Revolt of the Masses*. New York: Norton.
[3] Thomas Piketty (2014). *Capital in the Twenty-First Century*. Cambridge, MA: Belknap Press.

clear is that the technology giants, which are mainly interested in shareholder value, cannot really be trusted to be the arbiter of what are facts and what has been described as being "factoids." Unlike the more traditional media outlets—while using the cover of freedom of speech—they have been highly irresponsible in the matter of fact checking. Thus, given the power of the social media, the formation of public opinion seems to be out of control. It has become too easy to spread false information. New information technologies—given the editor-free world of the internet—are undermining the advantages that democracies once enjoyed over autocracy.

Of course, before the existence of the internet, there were always people who would spread false information. Presently, however, it has become much easier for likeminded people to find each other. In fact, the greatest threat to democracy is no longer censorship—the endangerment of people's free speech—but deliberate disinformation aimed at destabilizing democratic institutions and civic competence. Against the power and capacity of the social media, there exists a lack of trustworthy and trusted intermediate institutions capable of guarding knowledge production and dissemination. Without these institutions, the digital public sphere that's purely commercially driven does not serve democracy well. As a result, cyberspace has turned out to be a fantastic vehicle for populist demagogue-like leaders to create "alternative realities," thereby helping to facilitate regressive crowd-like behavior. After all, to be a keyboard warrior is so much easier than standing on the barricades. It takes much less courage to rally the troops from a distance.

Healthy societies and organizations, however, need people who aren't swept away by regressive crowd behavior. They need people who are able to maintain their sense of individuality in spite of the many pressures that could lead them to dissolving their conscience within a crowd. I am referring to people—taking a mental health perspective—who are prepared to engage in regular self-examination, people who are constantly asking themselves whether they still have a sufficient grip on reality. Just as in the ancient fairy tale about the Emperor's New Clothes, modern society always needs "little-boys-or-little-girls-in-the-crowd" who are willing to shout out that "the Emperor has no clothes."

In most Western societies, notwithstanding the efforts of these populist demagogue-like leaders, democratic institutions have still proven to be robust enough to prevent populism from descending into autocracy and totalitarianism. At the same time, without any doubt, given the efforts of these populist leaders, the quality of democracy has been negatively affected. Many of the political programs launched by these populists are soaked with nationalistic and xenophobic rhetoric and their activities have left a negative stamp on democracies. And although, as of yet, it hasn't destroyed democratic institutions, much damage has been done. Clearly, given the delicate nature of liberal democracies, not much is needed to cause a decrease in civil liberties. Democracy is always going to be a very fragile construction. Given the present worldwide developments, what's there for all to see is how leadership practices in many countries—the pandemic another contributing factor—have taken a great leap backward. From believing in the importance of institutional checks and balances, these countries have tumbled into the familiar territory of autocracy.

In more ways than one, this danger of an "inner rot" came home to me again while looking at Leni Riefenstahl's film about Hitler. Not only did the film make me squirm, but it also became a somewhat "aha" experience. The reason is that I found too many similarities between Donald Trump's populist theatrics and the histrionic behavior of Hitler. Studying the rallies of Trump and the behavior of his MAGA followers, I was struck by a sad reminder of how easily people can be seduced—how easily regressive crowd behavior can come to the fore. Clearly, Trump has been a grandmaster in creating "fan facts." In rallying his fans, he knows how to tell his "groupies" what they like to hear. What's also quite clear, given his extreme neediness, is the fact that these rallies seemed to be like oxygen to him. Narcissistically challenged people like Trump have an incessant hunger for affirmation from the crowd. Given their fragile sense of self-esteem, they require their regular "fix" of admiration through which they further descend into this Faustian pact with their followers.

Stepping on the podium, Trump would project the image of a happy warrior regaling big crowds with bogus conspiracy theories and his own distorted brand of humor. Whatever nonsense he would utter, his base remained loyal to the end with cheers, merriment, and chants of "Four more years!", "Lock them up!", "Build that wall!", "Stop the steal!". As in the case of Hitler, every lie would be swallowed as being an absolute truth. Of course, the ultimate lie would be the delusion that he had won the election, a reaction that's quite understandable. For a person with his kind of malignant narcissistic personality makeup, it would be completely unimaginable to ever lose. A person like Trump always needs to be a "winner." Every "loss" needs to be reframed as being a plot by this malicious, evil elite. Yet while going through these demagogic antics, he ignored a raging pandemic, a refusal that would cost the lives of hundreds of thousands of people. For Trump, however, that would be the least of his worries, given his complete self-centeredness. Perhaps, he overheard the statement of Josef Stalin who once allegedly said: "The death of one man is a tragedy. The death of millions is a statistic." For a person of his ilk, concepts like having a conscience, empathy, and compassion are far outside of his range of comprehension.

Crowd Psychology

In fact, the kind of crowd behavior seen in the rallies of Hitler and Trump has a long history. Taking an evolutionary perspective, these gatherings of crowds or "herding" behavior have always been a chosen activity in the animal kingdom, the human animal being no exception. It is quite clear that people like to amass in groups as a way of finding safety.

The Selfish Herd

With respect to such groupings, a "selfish herd" theory has been proposed, suggesting that herds come about as the result of complex spatial maneuvers whereby each individual in the herd is trying to ensure that another member of its species—in situations of imminent threats to life—will be the one eaten by predators.[4] And as is to be expected, in most social aggregations, the risk of predation will be higher at the periphery than at its center. Thus, a herd's fluid forms and movements are the outcome of having numerous individuals competing to stay close to its center, hoping that the other members of its species will end up between themselves and possible predators. In addition, to further understand this herdlike behavior—again taking an evolutionary perspective—we also need to consider the idea of information access. By aggregating in groups, it's likely that each member will benefit more easily from the knowledge gained by other group members, an important piece of information being the location of key resources. Again, evolution-wise, herding may help improve the foraging success of each individual.

Mimicry

Evolutionary or not, it is clear that being in a crowd can have a strange effect on human beings, especially on an emotional level. When assembled in a crowd, its members tend to reinforce each other's behavior through the process

---
[4] William Hamilton (1971). Geometry for the selfish herd, *Journal of Theoretical Biology*. 31, 295–311.

of mutual identification. Thus, emotional contagion—the phenomenon that individuals tend to express and feel emotions that are similar to those of others—can be viewed as another salient characteristic of *Homo sapiens*. We tend to mirror other people's emotional states. Once more, we can observe strong parallels between the behavior of herding animals and the activities of human crowds, for which Hitler's and Trump's rallies can serve as disturbing examples. As suggested earlier, particularly in situations of danger, copying what other people are doing can be a highly effective survival strategy. Often, it can be a lifeline to safety. Clearly, a degree of mimicry seems to be ingrained into our DNA.

In fact, our capacity for mimicry is very well illustrated by the behavior of infants. From a very early stage in life, they can be observed mimicking emotions of their caregivers.[5] And all through life, this proclivity toward emotional contagion will remain. This kind of hardwiring explains *Homo sapiens*' strange behavior at human gatherings, where we can observe large groups of people acting in the same way, at the same time. Clearly, as I suggested before, the frenzy of members of a crowd can be contagious, pointing out that this kind of contagion will feed upon itself. Unfortunately, the kinds of behaviors that enable the wisdom of crowds can also contribute to very erratic, even insane, behavior—the rallies of Hitler and Trump being prime examples.

From a neurological perspective, an explanation for this strange behavior can be given by introducing the concept of mirror neurons. I am referring to the existence of visuospatial neurons, which seem to influence human social interaction. To elaborate, researchers studying the brains of macaque monkeys discovered that certain neurons started firing when the monkeys did something and when they watched other monkeys doing the same thing. These animal behavior studies led to the observation that mirror neurons are the fundamental building blocks of mimicry and emotional contagion. According to these researchers, it is these specific neurons that make us social creatures, impacting every aspect of how we interact with others, including the processing of information.[6] The presence of these mirror neurons has led to new ways of thinking about how we generate our own actions and how we monitor and interpret the actions of others.

---

[5] Susan S. Jones (2007). Imitation in infancy: The development of mimicry, *Psychological Science*. 18 (7), 593–599.
[6] Giacomo Rizzolatti and Maddalena Fabbri-Destro (2008). The mirror system and its role in social cognition, *Current Opinion in Neurobiology*. 18 (2), 179–184.

Psychological Explanations

If these various theories aren't enough to explain the "madness of crowds," then turning from the evolutionary-neurological sphere to the psychological one should surely help to complete the picture. As is well known, social-psychological pressures can create the need in human beings to fit in. I am referring to the influence of social conformity.[7] This pressure to conform is in response to real (involving the physical presence of others) or imagined (involving the pressure of social norms/expectations) group pressures. In other words, conformity can be defined as yielding to group pressures, something which nearly all of us will do at times. Thus, to put it in another way, social pressures toward conformity in thinking and acting are also very much a part of our species' heritage. It can be seen as an inevitable derivative of the kind of herd behavior mentioned earlier.

We may recall how in situations where we are unsure of the correct response, we often look to others who appear to be better informed and more knowledgeable. We use their lead as a guide for our own behavior. In addition, the reason we behave in specific ways could also be due to the need to avoid punishments, which is further related to social conformity. As a result, we feel forced to go along with certain kinds of behavior, even though we may disagree with it. Finally, social conformity could also be the result of the wish to gain rewards, such as behaving in a certain manner in order to get other people to like us.

In searching for other explanations of the strange behavior of crowds, another psychological dynamic worth mentioning is a process called the "idealizing" and "mirror" transference, concepts well known in the psychoanalytical literature.[8] Given prevailing clinical observations, transference reactions are seen as occurring when people redirect some of their emotional reactions toward others to an entirely different person. In the case of these strange interpersonal processes, the other person—usually a person in a position of power and authority—is often experienced as a powerful, omniscient parental figure.

People who resort to "idealizing" the other feel protected and imagine that they are able to share in the power and capabilities of the person they look up to, very similarly to the way a young child idealizes his or her parents and feels protected by

---

[7] Solomon E. Asch (1948). The doctrine of suggestion, prestige and imitation in social psychology, *Psychological Review*. 55 (5), 250–276.

[8] Sigmund Freud (1905). Fragment of an Analysis of a Case of Hysteria, in *The Standard Edition of the Complete Psychological Works of Sigmund Freud*, VII, ed. J. Strachey. London: Hogarth Press; Heinz Kohut (1968). The Psychoanalytic Treatment of Narcissistic Personality Disorders. In *The Search for the Self* (Vol. I), pp. 477–509. New York: International Universities Press.

them. Naturally, people in leadership positions—such as authority figures—quite easily take on this role. Intrapsychically, the person in the thralls of these transferential processes embarks on a reasoning process that goes as follows: "You appear to be perfect, thus, I want to be a part of you."

We can see how, quite often, populist-like movements are led by charismatic-like, narcissistic figures who present themselves as the "voice of the people." Such leaders campaign and attract support on the basis of their own personal appeal. Given their antics, which are helped by these transferential idealization processes, people can easily identify with what they pretend to stand for. It is yet another explanation for the strange psychological dynamics that can be found within crowds. We can observe how its members imagine that they have a personal connection with the leader. In their imagination, they will try to incorporate aspects of the leader within themselves—to have the narcissistic fantasy that they are like the leader.[9] And this connection seems to go both ways. Likewise, these populist leaders claim that they have a direct relationship with "the people," even imagining themselves to be the personification of their wishes.

This interactive transferential process illustrates the need of human beings to maintain some kind of narcissistic fusion with people in power and authority due to experienced feelings of powerlessness. Conversely, the person who receives these projections will be the recipient of this transferential "mirroring process" due to the admiration of these people. Consequently, for both parties, it creates a mutually fulfilling but macabre "dance" that doesn't suggest mature behavior. On the contrary, it is indicative of some kind of group regression, a resorting to childlike behavior. At the same time, being part of a group also offers a reparative and substitutive function, particularly to people who are looking for an idealized leader to repair a sense of self that has been experienced as defective. As suggested before, to deal with feelings of helplessness, they imagine that aspects of the leader's power will be transferred to them.

In addition, what makes them feel less helpless is a sense that they're not alone. There are others who are in the same boat—others they can identify with, which makes them feel stronger. Thus, identification with the leader—and with each other—will be an antidote to their feelings of helplessness. At the same time, as suggested before, while being part of this strange "dance," the members of the group are catering to the leader's narcissistic needs. Once

---

[9] Sigmund Freud (1930/2001). *Civilization and Its Discontents, The Standard Edition of the Complete Psychological Works of Sigmund Freud, XXI*. ed. J. Strachey. London: Hogarth Press.

they are a part of this dance, however, anything goes. Morality and ethical considerations evaporate. Any untruth is reframed as a hard fact.

Given these intricate group dynamics that very much come to the fore in the film *Triumph of the Will*, we may now be able to better understand how these populist leaders are taking advantage of crowd psychology, and how they are able to use these processes to benefit their own, often dark ends. These dynamics and the associated theories also shed light on how crowds themselves can exert a strange psychological influence on their members, Leni Riefenstahl's film being an outstanding example of these regressive processes.

It is for all to see how the Nazi audience's critical faculties were swept away when Hitler used to talk. Every untruth the Führer pronounced appeared to be accepted as a godlike axiom due to his talent in "hypnotizing" his audience. And while he was telling them all these "fan facts"—the things that his fans would like to hear—he was really creating an alternative reality. Thus, sadly enough, while he was doing what he was doing, his fans appeared to become transformed into members of a cult. When cultlike behavior comes to the fore, anything goes; anything is believed. And the atrocities instigated by Hitler during World War II are terrifying signifiers of the after-effects of these dangerous ideologies. Certainly, the historical precedent set by Hitler and his followers creates serious concerns about what some of Trump's followers would be capable of. In spite of Trump having lost the election, they continue to believe in an alternative reality, egged on by his actions.

Dissolving the Conscience

We can see how the hypnotizing influence of a leader, combined with the anonymity of belonging to a large group of people, can lead to highly irrational, emotionally charged behavior. Once more, taking a closer look at Leni Riefenstahl's film, it becomes quickly apparent that the participants at this Nazi rally seemed to have lost control of their personal values and standards. Whatever dangerous nonsense Hitler was espousing, it was internalized as the absolute truth. Clearly, his "groupies" seemed no longer able to judge what is and what isn't appropriate behavior. Subsequently, their internal and social standards dropped by the wayside, and they began to behave in a more primitive, regressive manner. These are the same patterns evident in other large groups that have become intoxicated by such leaders.

What we see is that among these groupings, the leader takes over its members' critical functions, relieving them of any personal responsibility. Instead, they let their leader—in this case Hitler—take over their conscience. This explains why anything that he tells his audience appears to be lapped up as an absolute truth. As the audience becomes less controlled in their behavior, they simply go along with whatever "truth" is suggested to them. It explains the element of drama almost invariably present in these "mass" groupings, whether in the form of bizarre behavior, exaggerated emotionality, easy acceptance of extremist ideologies, and even expression of violence.

Furthermore, the experience of being anonymous within a crowd also lessens these people's concerns with social standards, lowering the threshold to engage in antisocial kinds of behaviors. Often, as time goes by, the members of such crowds become both more uncontrolled and more willing to behave in an antisocial manner. Due to the fact that their leader has taken over their critical faculties, the members of the crowd become incapable of reasoning rationally, demonstrating a great lack of judgment and critical thinking.

When a group turns into some kind of cult, its truths become a central source of meaning and self-definition.[10] At these gatherings, alternative realities are created. Whatever the real facts are, they are discarded. Any lie or "alternative fact" becomes the new truth. And, given their strong identification with the leader, the followers believe anything that's being said in spite of overwhelming evidence to the contrary. Clearly, when we enter the domain of cultlike behavior, real facts are no longer of any importance. And although Hitler may be an extremely dark example, much of Trump's behavior has followed a similar pattern. He has become a contemporary magician capable of creating alternative realities. Unfortunately, many other national leaders have been following his disturbing example.

The Sycophant Effects

What's also interesting to observe in this dance between leader and followers is the sycophant effect, whereby followers, due to their strong identification with their leader, are prepared to accept everything that's being said. This process is reflected most keenly in the behavior of these leaders' inner circles, which often function like an echo chamber. These people ensure that these leaders only hear what they like to hear. They begin to serve as "filters" to prevent any unwelcome news reaching the ears of the leader since they are fearful of possibly igniting the leader's narcissistic rage.

---

[10] Manfred F. R. Kets de Vries (2020). *The CEO Whisperer: Meditations on Leaders, Life and Change*. London: Palgrave Macmillan.

People like Hitler and Trump would never have been able to do what they have been doing, without an army of these sycophantic "enablers"—people whose behavior helps the leader to continue with their destructive behavior patterns. Most often, the people in authority to whom these sycophantic enablers suck up to have a narcissistic personality, and thus require endless approval from their followers. They need to be constantly told that they are like god's gift to humankind. The slightest bit of criticism or dissent, however, will be interpreted as a hostile act, being experienced as a narcissistic injury that can lead to an attack of rage. This fear is sufficient to keep the followers of these kinds of leaders in line.

While narcissism is the predominant feature of these leaders, many of their sycophantic enablers have more of a dependent personality structure. These sycophants tend to search out people who they perceive possess power and authority. In fact, people with this mindset have a longstanding, persistent and inflexible pattern of wanting to rely on others for their emotional and physical needs. Given their dependency needs, these people are prepared to do anything to get along, to be viewed favorably by those in a position of power and authority. Given their personality structure, they are quite prepared to fit into the latest groupthink—to conform to whatever position is currently seen as being politically correct.[11] Of course, the excessive feelings of dependency of these people may lead to notably submissive and clingy behavior.

Given their lack of self-confidence, these people often don't really trust their own judgment. Typically, they defer to the person in charge when faced with making decisions. The idea of expressing criticism rarely comes to mind, fearful that it would jeopardize their closeness to the leader. Instead, these sycophantic enablers are quick to criticize or attack those who dare to question the existing groupthink or, even worse in the enabler's mind, dare to undermine the revered leader. Unfortunately, it is exactly this kind of behavior that facilitates this terrifying enabling process.

Much of this kind of behavior can be observed in countries where populist-like leaders have attained power. And as I mentioned before, such behavior tends to be a mutually reinforcing dance as both parties may not recognize that there's a problem. Of course, there are going to be instances where some of them may silently disagree with what's happening but are too anxious to speak up—they are reluctant to express that there's a problem. Fearful of being subjected to the wrath of the leader, they prefer to play it safe. But as a

---

[11] Irving L. Janis (1982). *Groupthink: Psychological Studies of Policy Decisions and Fiascoes* (2nd ed.). Boston: Cengage Learning.

way to absolve their conscience, they're often quite talented in rationalizing their lack of action. Of course, some of these people could be making a more opportunistic choice. They may like being close to the sources of power and the "goodies"—in the form of power, status, and wealth—that may come their way.

Unfortunately, given the way these people behave, it sends out the message to others that there's nothing wrong with what they're doing. By not acknowledging that there is a problem, they enable these leaders to continue their harmful ways without experiencing any of the consequences. In that respect, we can only imagine the kinds of conversations that are taking place around leaders such as Xi Jinping of China, Kim Jong-un of North Korea, Paul Kagame of Rwanda, or Recep Tayyip Erdoğan of Turkey. The question is what kind of world are these people creating? Will it be a meaningful one for the people who live in it? After all, one of the major existential needs for all human beings is "to own your own life!"

My thoughts about the dangers of toxic leadership brought me to the disturbing societal trend of having leaders for life. Given my concerns about this unfortunate development, my mind drifted off, reflecting on what could be said about it. It made me think of the "modest proposal" once written by the satirist and essayist Jonathan Swift. In his famous essay, as a way of commenting on the worsening conditions in Ireland, he made the outrageous suggestion that the impoverished Irish might be able to ease their economic troubles by selling their children as food to rich gentlemen and ladies. In reality, what Swift sought to do in this satirical presentation was to relentlessly mock the heartless attitudes displayed by the British at that time vis-à-vis the poor, as well as their dealings with the Irish in general. It made me wonder why I shouldn't write something similar, mocking the kinds of leaders who try to hang onto their positions for life. What comments could I make to condemn their autocratic practices? Upon further reflection, I thought that satire might also be the best way to expose the danger of this kind of *modus operandi*.

2

Let's Install Leaders for Life

Power tends to corrupt; absolute power corrupts absolutely.
—Lord Acton

There are no beautiful surfaces without a terrible depth.
—Friedrich Nietzsche

A "Swiftian" Proposal

It is with great joy and heartfelt satisfaction that I am finally witnessing the idea of "leaders for life" gaining real traction in our world and I have to say I'm over the moon about it. I must admit I was worried for a while, thinking that this concept had become a thing of the past. But on seeing so many contemporary leaders—among them Xi Jinping and Vladimir Putin—boldly recognize its obvious merits and work tirelessly to install themselves as lifetime leaders, I can't help but breathe a sigh of relief.

Perhaps, what has made a real difference is the renewed life and unique "flare" that many of these visionary leaders have brought to the effort. Of course, a prime example is the earlier mentioned Donald J. Trump of "making America great again" fame. Not long after his inauguration, he already recognized the great benefits of having leaders for life. It was so encouraging, when in March 2018—while addressing a crowd of donors at his Florida estate—he offered unabashed praise for China's new constitutional amendment removing presidential term limits and allowing Xi Jinping to serve in that office indefinitely. Talking about Xi, Trump said in his rich vocabulary, as perceptive as he always can be: "He's now president for life, president for life. And he's great. And look, he was able to do that. I think it's great. Maybe we'll have to give it a shot someday."[1]

He couldn't have been closer to the truth. After all, the Chinese have been imitating the Americans all these years. Isn't it time for Americans to begin imitating the Chinese? Who knows, having a president for life—Trump truly would have been a dream candidate—would really make America great again. In his case, he really tried, but sadly failed. It's heartbreaking. The silent majority can be so ungrateful!

I strongly believe, at a time when the mistrust of politicians in liberal democracies has reached astronomical heights, there is no question, having strongman leaders is going to be the answer. How much more preferable it would be to have them in power compared to these wishy-washy leaders in the so-called liberal democracies. At least, leaders for life give the populace the feeling that there is somebody in charge, somebody willing to protect them. And even if that turns out to be a massive illusion, who cares, right? When I compare the behavior of these leaders with the tricky political games played by many of those alleged democratic politicians, I'm all the more convinced that this leaders-for-life approach is so much better. The great benefits we sow from stability should never be underestimated. It is what makes having leaders for life such a great proposition.

Time-Limited Leaders Akin to "Post Turtles"

Let's pause and carefully consider what's wrong with these time-limited leaders. As far as I'm concerned, they are nothing more than "post turtles." And what do I mean by that? Imagine you're driving on a country road. All of a sudden, you see a turtle balancing on a fence post. Obviously, it didn't get up there by itself. And naturally, it doesn't belong there. Add to this that it doesn't know what to do while it is up there, as it is elevated beyond its ability to function. Furthermore, what you may also be asking yourself is what kind of idiot would put this turtle there in the first place. That's the problem with many of these temporary leaders of these supposed liberal democracies. They are often not fit for the job. And the populace doesn't even realize the dismal outcome that awaits them when they elect these people. Their time horizon is just too short to get anything meaningful done. Given their limited tenures, they will

---

[1] https://www.theguardian.com/us-news/2018/mar/04/donald-trump-praises-xi-jinping-power-grab-give-that-a-shot-china.

never be experienced enough to do so. They're like Alice in Wonderland, just stumbling around, not knowing where they will end up.

Instead, having a leader for life creates the kind of political and policy continuity that most of us are always craving or dreaming of. It is very comforting to have the same person in charge of the affairs of state. It's been long known that a sense of permanence creates feelings of safety. Like in the case with monarchies, it gives us somebody to identify with. Isn't it crystal clear that these continual changes of people in leadership positions are far too disruptive? Often, it is just a prescription for chaos. Let's be honest, the idea of building an inclusive political system that represents the interests of every citizen is nothing but a pipe dream. Finding people who are seriously committed to democratic political and legal institutions, who believe in the value of open debate, who have a desire to create a society that makes it possible for each citizen to lead a fulfilling life, and who want to create an economy that allows its citizens and their institutions to flourish—that's going to be impossible. Most people in the know have come to realize that democracy in itself is an incredibly unstable system of government. It is far too dependent on the whims and caprices of the general public, people who for the most part are quite ignorant of what's needed to govern well. Far too often, we can see that the changes these liberal democrats are demanding undermine what is already a very well-running machine.

Absolute Power Is Kind of Neat

Should we be troubled by the statement that "absolute power corrupts absolutely?" To be direct: no. When you think about it, what's so bad about having some power? Even a lot of power? After all, only through power do things get done. Furthermore, there are always going to be occasions when force is required to keep a population in line. That's just how it is. Ignorant as the masses tend to be, they can at times become quite unreasonable and even unruly. It's just good business to clamp down and bring them under control. And in the context of power, why be so negative about using the word "corruption?" Shouldn't we just accept it as part of the human condition? Isn't it the inevitable glue that keeps most societies functioning? So, in sum, power, corruption, force, these are the building blocks—the "ABCs"—of a great society, and it's time we recognized that.

All of this becomes clearer when we reflect back on our history.

From Paleolithic times, *Homo sapiens* have always been looking for leaders who provide stability. They have wanted the kinds of people in charge who they could look up to, who would tell them what to do. That these leaders acquire power is only par for the course. Given the evolutionary makeup of human beings, I do think that the concerns some people have about leaders gaining too much power and staying in office too long are highly exaggerated. And this whole idea that the personalization of governmental rule facilitates the abuse of power is just a bunch of hearsay. Generally speaking, a population is in great need of role models. To suggest that there is a strong correlation between entrenched leadership and the economic and social decline of a country is a regrettable exaggeration. After all, hasn't it been said that there are three kinds of lies: lies, damned lies, and statistics?

A Glorious History of "Leaders for Life"—Caesar, Napoleon, Ceaușescu, and Hitler

Actually, many people don't realize that the idea of having leaders for life has such a glorious history. Just think of Julius Caesar who, in 45 BC, appointed himself as "Perpetual Dictator." Notwithstanding his truly unfortunate end, it was Caesar's example that inspired—after his assassination—a string of Roman emperors to aim for a similar position. Being the real path breaker that Caesar turned out to be, he came to be copied by Napoleon Bonaparte, who in 1802 was appointed "First Consul for Life" before elevating himself two years later to the rank of Emperor. Actually, to give himself the title of Emperor made him truly a trendsetter. It turned him into a role model for many others, including Jean-Bédel Bokassa, known as Bokassa I of the Central African Republic, another visionary leader who also had the audacity and brilliance to crown himself Emperor. Original as he was in the way he was running his country—let's ignore his dabbling in cannibalism—I can imagine that many visionary people think it to be highly regrettable that he was overthrown in a coup. Also, from what I have understood, many people saw it as quite unfair that his people tried him and sentenced him to death for treason and murder. Fortunately, later on, his death sentence was commuted to life in solitary confinement.

It still saddens me to know that Nicolae Ceaușescu, the leader of Romania from 1965 to 1989, was less fortunate. In spite of the exemplary way the *conducător*, as he always liked to call himself, had been running the country, in the end he and his wife faced some kind of kangaroo court that sentenced them to death, calling for their immediate execution. One cannot but agree that it was a shameful end for a man who had done so much for his country.

I still wonder why it all had to happen because, just before his death, Ceaușescu gave a visionary speech praising the achievements of the "socialist revolution" and Romania's "multi-laterally developed socialist society." As he explained, whatever rioting against his rule was taking place, it was all caused by "fascist agitators who were trying to destroy socialism." It is truly remarkable how ungrateful people can be!

Of course, as already discussed, another great example of a leader for life would have been Adolf Hitler, the person who was a role model in the previous chapter. I must admit that I am somewhat hesitant to advocate for his case, realizing that by invoking his name I may well elicit the view that he is less than an ideal example. But he certainly has earned an infamous place in history. Think of it: after being appointed Chancellor of Germany, the German Reichstag voted to merge the offices of President and Chancellor, giving Hitler the title of Führer—the almighty leader. Soon after, the Reichstag voted to allow Hitler to hold the positions of Chancellor and Führer for life. And I do believe that there are still some people out there who think that it has been truly unfortunate that things didn't work out so well. But as Joseph Stalin, another great leader for life of the USSR, once said quite accurately, "[y]ou cannot make a revolution with silk gloves." Another of this great man's astute observations was: "People who cast the votes decide nothing. The people who count the votes decide everything!"

Mugabe and Mobutu—Also Making Their Countries "Great Again"

Other exemplary leaders worth mentioning must have been inspired by these great role models. Take, for example, Robert Mugabe, another truly visionary leader who selflessly volunteered to become his country's leader for life. In his very inspiring, singular way, he was yet another leader trying to make his country great again. I can only say how unfortunate it must have been that he didn't completely succeed in his mission. Obviously, the blame has to be placed on the demonical efforts of the many Western countries that sabotaged this great man's "good works." How mistaken they were to suggest that under his rule, Zimbabwe—according to them once one of the African continent's richest countries—became a place of chronic underdevelopment with a totally decrepit economy. Preposterous as it may sound, they suggested that during his time in office, there was a dramatic drop in life expectancy and per capita income. They even mentioned that due to his reign, the country became the world champion in hyperinflation. It is just incredible to what lengths some people will go in their defamatory efforts. Fortunately, and very correctly, Mugabe would call the push for term limits a "Western attempt to place a yoke around the necks of African leaders."[2] Insightful as he always has been, he really hit the nail on the head.

Of course, I have always been intrigued by the way President Mobutu Sese Seko of the Democratic Republic of the Congo (DRC) was able to build such a great country. Unfortunately, the press was totally against him and that has left him truly misunderstood. For example, is it really credible that under his three-decade-long enlightened leadership the DRC suffered from gross corruption, embezzlement, and neglect of the public infrastructure? Is it also credible that an economy based almost exclusively on mineral extraction deteriorated as Mobutu forced out foreign-owned companies and embezzled government funds? And is it also credible that his successors, first Laurent Kabila who overthrew him in 1997 (but was assassinated in 2001) and subsequently his son, Joseph, have been doing more of the same? Did they, like their predecessor, really amass a fortune by stealing state funds and effectively disregarding the provision of public services? Come on. It is completely clear to me that here, as with many other heroic leaders for life, we have been fed a bunch of lies.

Taking these great African leaders as role models, it is really heartwarming to see how President Yoweri Museveni of Uganda has been creatively holding on to power, having been declared victor of a sixth five-year term in office. The comment that his recent election had been unfair (a contention backed by supposedly independent international observers) is just another example of how low his contenders are willing to go. These people are just too negative. They keep on complaining about the corruption, chronic unemployment, and poor public services across the nation. But their comments can't be trusted. We all know that they're backed by foreign "agents" and "homosexuals." Clearly, they just want to start an insurrection that would create chaos across the country. Thus, given all these falsehoods, it was in the best interest of all to shut down the internet to save the population from all this false information. Also, to prevent rumor mongering, it was a sensible move to arrest the observers of the election. They are known for spreading false rumors. Just think about the lies they spread, saying that many people have been killed and arrested by the security forces.

---

[2] https://css.ethz.ch/en/services/digital-library/articles/article.html/513dbea7-2e06-47a6-b3f1-af8c1c86b419.

Turkmenbashi of Turkmenistan— A Narcissistic Visionary

I would be at fault not to give praise to the visionary activities of the late Turkmenbashi of Turkmenistan. Before he became president, this great leader's real name was Saparmurat Niyazov, but in renaming himself he made it quite clear that he was the head of all Turkmen. This president for life truly knew what needed to be done to make his country a shining example for other nations. And in making this assessment, I prefer to ignore the comments of some "spoilers," who have had the nerve to say that his actions were a little self-centered. Such talk is nothing but sour grapes. I have always believed that a solid dose of narcissism is nothing to be ashamed of. Actually, a leader's narcissism can be very helpful in making the people of a country proud again. Narcissism is such a marvelous engine to drive leaders to greater heights.

To emphasize this point, wasn't it thoughtful of Turkmenbashi to rename the town of Krasnovodsk after himself? Seemingly on a roll, he renamed the months of the year, schools, and airports also after himself, and generous as he could be, after the members of his family. I can only imagine that his country's citizens must have been so thrilled by all these changes. Obviously, they viewed it as a brilliant move, as it made it so much easier for them to remember what was truly important. Furthermore, I would like to add that this visionary leader, in trying to beautify the capital, erected a large, golden, rotating statue of himself. As a sign of Turkmenbashi's skill for always knowing what was in the best interest of his country, it turned into a remarkable tourist attraction. By the way, I should mention that I thought it to be in very bad taste that, after his death, his successor decided to topple the statue.

Enlightened as Turkmenbashi was, he wrote—or, perhaps better said, had written for him—*Ruhnama* [*The Book of the Soul*], an ideological treatise, in which he graciously offered spiritual and moral guidance to his people. How malicious it was that some people would say that he was quite illiterate. They just didn't appreciate his thoughtfulness at making the reading of the *Ruhnama* mandatory in schools, universities, and governmental organizations. It was a sign of his great foresight to have new governmental employees tested on their knowledge of the book at job interviews. Being the enlightened leader that he was, he went so far as to make sure it became part of the driver's license exam. What's more, some people whispered that Turkmenbashi had also interceded with God to ensure that any student who read the *Ruhnama* three times would automatically have a place in heaven. We should give him credit for really going out of his way to be a servant to his people.

Turkmenbashi also had the foresight to ban beards, ballet, playing the radio in cars, video games, and golden-capped teeth. Obviously, in the case of gold teeth, he must have seen it as a waste of possible "building material" that could have been put to so much better use by erecting more golden statues of himself. What's also very touching is how it was for all to see how much his people loved him. At any gathering that was honored by his presence, the most prominent people in the country would walk onto the stage to thank and praise him to the loud applause of the other people in the audience. Clearly, the rumors that this beloved president for life tortured people and sent dissidents to mental hospitals must have been complete slander.[3]

Kim Jong-un—Our Ultimate Role Model

The ultimate role model demonstrating the advantages of having leaders for life must be in North Korea. Realizing how beneficial such arrangements can be for everyone, the enlightened Kim family went one step further compared to most of these other visionary leaders for life. They managed to create a true president for life dynasty. After the death of Kim Il-sung, the first president for life, the North Korean government (being extremely respectful in commemorating the founder of the nation) decided to write the presidential office out of the constitution. They made him the "Eternal President" as a way of honoring his memory forever. Since then, Kim Il-sung's son and grandson have been presiding over the country. I think this highly innovative fashion of dealing with a country's leadership is truly a great way to go. It is also worth repeating that the legitimacy of its rulers has remained uncontested, helped by its unique official philosophy called "*juche*."

Perhaps the best way to describe the *juche* ideology is by substituting it for the word "self-reliance." From what I understand, this state ideology is a highly original blend of many different ideas, some borrowed from Marxism, while others come from Confucianism, twentieth-century Japanese imperialism, and traditional Korean nationalism. Using such ideas has really been a masterstroke. It ensured a leadership dynasty by advocating that the country must remain separate and distinct from the world, dependent solely on its own strength and, not to be forgotten, guidance from its deservedly revered, near-godlike leader.

---

[3] https://www.theguardian.com/world/2006/dec/21/1.

I strongly believe that the present supreme leader of North Korea, Kim Jong-un—guided by this unmatched ideology—is doing an incredible job. Take, for example, his rocket-building endeavors—they have become the envy of the world. In addition, being the great innovator that he truly is, he has come up with new ways to leverage the political power of developing nuclear weapons. To call what he is doing a malignant form of blackmail is so far from the truth. In fact, he is really an innovator, contributing to the technological advancements of his country. Given his remarkable achievements, it is hard to understand why some people complain about the country's starving population, its use of slave labor, and, allegedly, the presence of unspeakable detention camps. The comments made by those critical of the enlightened Kim regime that the alleged atrocities in its prisons are even worse than what happened in the Nazi concentration camps cannot be but malicious propaganda.

The Democratic Delusion

Still, I find it deeply regrettable that many of the leaders who have had the courage to proclaim themselves leaders for life have not always been successful in serving out their life term. At times, sadly enough, their own citizens have made it very difficult for them to hang on to their position. Obviously, their subjects never realized what's good for their own country. What is a real disgrace is that many of these leaders for life have been deposed long before their death, while others truly fulfilled their title by being assassinated while in office. But it is also very gratifying to know that some managed to hang in there until their natural death. After all, to be assassinated doesn't set a very good example. It doesn't make for good public relations.

To clarify my position once more, I am of the belief that it doesn't make very much sense to put into place constitutional provisions on term limits, which would suggest that no leader is indispensable. There is something to be said about indispensability. In the world we live in, with all its democratic demagoguery, it is more important than ever before to maintain stability at all costs. To aim for continuity is part of the natural order. It assures that everyone knows his or her place in the general scheme of things. For the populace at large, it is beneficial to have a leader who they can look up to as the protector of the nation—the kind of leader who offers them a feeling of safety.

A country's citizens should count their blessings to have leaders for life. Given the many benefits these leaders for life can bring to a country, there will be times when it becomes imperative to resort to more subtle ways for assuring lifelong positions. Unfortunately, however, in this day and age, it has become more difficult to be such a leader. Often, aspiring leaders for life have to deal with citizens who have strange ideas about the imagined blessings of a liberal democracy. Given what some of these leaders are up against, I have great admiration for the way many of them manage to overcome the resistances of these very negative people. What's encouraging is that many of these leaders have found highly creative ways to make their wishes turn into reality. Some of them are extremely creative in finding ways to stay in power.

Thus, I am happy to say that leader-term-limit evasion is really picking up. Presently, it is very gratifying to see that about one-third of all leaders who reach the end of their term are making serious attempts to overstay their duration. And isn't it great that two-thirds of them, while making these attempts, are successful?[4]

Creative Election Strategies

In the world we live in, many of these innovative leaders have also realized that for the sake of appearances it can be in poor taste to aim explicitly for officially granted life terms. Unfortunately, the way things are, if they want to hold on to their position, they have sometimes no choice but to become more sophisticated and even legalistic in the ways to go about it. Nowadays, to merely resort to brute force to stay in power seems to be somewhat passé. Sadly enough, banning opposition parties, dismissing the legislature, locking up or even eliminating opponents doesn't always make for good image management.

Managed Elections

Fortunately, many of these leaders for life have become much more ingenious in their efforts to creatively use "legal" means to subvert what can be quite tiresome constitutional constraints to their stay in power. For example, what has proven to be a highly effective approach to assure lifelong positions is to have periodic renewals of a leadership mandate through "friendly," what some people call "managed," elections. For example, many of these deserving leaders have discovered that it can be very effective to give "handouts"—malicious people have the nerve to call it bribes—just before elections. In most cases, it

---

[4] https://papers.ssrn.com/sol3/papers.cfm?abstract_id=3359960.

helps ensure that the candidate obtains high levels of support. (Of course, I think, if possible, candidates should always aim for a hundred percent support.) What also helps is to create "friendly," strategically guided opposition groups. At least, it gives possible troublemakers the illusion that they have a choice between different candidates.

It is quite laughable how far off the mark critics are when they complain about these leaders illegally using constitutional amendments. What's really so bad about rewriting the constitution, or even using the courts to reinterpret the constitution? After all, as I suggested before, leaders who have these long-term time horizons do know what's in the best interests of their countries. All in all, resorting to more constitutional types of coups is a great way to go if you're aiming to assure for yourself a leader-for-life position when you know what's the best for a country. Such innovative interventions enable these enlightened leaders to reframe the constitution by making subtler changes, with the ultimate purpose of preventing their removal from office. I find it a very creative way to assure continuity.

For example, Alexander Lukashenko of Belarus, the former Soviet farm boss, has been highly successful in his managed election efforts by winning a sixth term. The stability he has created for his country being in power since 1994 is unmatched. Unfortunately, during the most recent election, he seemed to have been too kind, having claimed his victory by only 80% of the votes. Why he didn't claim a 99% success rate is really a mystery to me. In spite of his impressive peace-making gestures, he had to deal with mass protests against his rule. Why the population in Belarus fails to realize how blessed they are to have such an enlightened leader is truly a great tragedy. He has always been such a great force for stability in the country, succeeding in his efforts to maintain an orderly Soviet-like regime. Fortunately, his powerful secret police, still called the KGB, have been rightly monitoring all troublemakers, throwing them in jail, and (which must be a false accusation) also torturing them. Sadly enough, there is so much ingratitude in life.

To switch continents, I have always looked up to President Paul Kagame of Rwanda as an outstanding role model when it comes to managed elections. He truly has a deep knowledge of what it takes to hang on to power. Presently, due to his very creative constitutional interventions, he will be able to stay in office until 2034, while at the same time preserving the fantasy of some kind of democratic legitimacy. In addition, former Sudanese president Omar al-Bashir should be seen as another leader who had been highly creative in constitutional obfuscation. In his case, however, it has been very unfortunate that he had a few misunderstandings with his citizens, which resulted in him becoming the victim of a coup.

And while we are at it, let us not forget to mention President Daniel Ortega of Nicaragua, a master in using the country's judicial system for getting what he wants—in other words, succeeding to stay on for life. Furthermore, I also very much admire the creative efforts of Hun Sen of Cambodia, now having become the longest-serving head of government, and one of the longest-serving leaders in the world. He always seemed to have a great way with political opponents. The accusation that under his rule, thousands of opposition activists, politicians, and human rights workers have been murdered must be completely untrue. In addition, I should not forget to mention that Nicolás Maduro, the president of Venezuela—like his predecessor Hugo Chávez—hasn't been a slouch when it comes to these innovative affairs of state. Furthermore, it is also very comforting to know that Abdel Fattah el-Sisi of Egypt is well on his way to becoming a president for life, reinstating an admirable country tradition. And isn't it nice—if the rumors are correct—that, like his predecessor Hosni Mubarak, he is preparing his eldest son to take over the reins?

The Need for a Coup

Of course, there are still going to be a few occasions when a coup is warranted. A shining example illustrating the need for a coup can be seen in Myanmar. Obviously, the country was going to pot when it tried to become more democratic. Fortunately, its enlightened generals saw it coming. They realized that a democratic wave would endanger the highly efficient ways they had been running their elaborate business conglomerates. Obviously, they realized that if they would no longer be in charge, how would they be able to afford all the weaponry needed to keep their citizens in line? Also, I can imagine that as a general, keeping up with the other generals doesn't come cheap. You better keep the money flowing. Therefore, hasn't it been remarkable how their brave soldiers, only armed with automatic weapons, were able to defend themselves against these vicious rock-throwing teenagers? Yes, I have heard that there were a few casualties, but when you make an omelet, a few eggs will be broken. However, what are a few lives lost in comparison to having a stable country?

The Proxy President Innovation

Actually, a brilliant method for ensuring presidencies for life—making President Vladimir Putin again an outstanding role model—is to appoint a placeholder president. I always thought it to be a complete disgrace that Russian presidents were limited to only two consecutive terms of four years. Therefore, it was so pleasing to see how Putin endorsed his handpicked successor, Dmitry Medvedev, as a temporary president. It enabled him to pick up the presidency once more afterward—and eventually to reform the constitution. Wasn't it heartening that this "father of the nation" achieved 78% support for his constitutional reform package? Of course, what must have been of great help to him was packaging the change in term limits within 200 other amendments. Surely, Putin is a person who knows how to innovate! I can only add that, by hanging in there, it is certain that he will do more great things for his country. His past history has shown that he really knows how to obtain global respect. That he has been poisoning adversaries with *novichok* must be a vicious lie. As a matter of fact, his support for Bashar al-Assad of Syria, another president for life, demonstrates his admirable way of going about things. That al-Assad uses brutal security services, torture chambers, and has created a culture of fear and repression must merely be hearsay. I think that this president for life is only continuing the glorious tradition of his father, Hafez al-Assad, also such an experienced leader for life, and who, like his son, ran his country in such an enlightened way. Who can ever forget how gloriously Bashar's father put down a Muslim brotherhood uprising in Hama by bulldozing the city, an act badmouthed as one of the deadliest acts by any Arab government against its own people in the modern Middle East? Truth be spoken, it must be a lie that tens of thousands of people died, and that Assad's father was giving the following message: don't mess with this regime or we will bury you all. Clearly, it must also be another act of foul-mouthing to say that his son has in masterly fashion outperformed his father in these matters.

Coming back to the institution of proxy presidencies, it seems to be not only popular in Russia but particularly in South America. For example, when Luis Arce took office as Bolivia's president following his clear victory, the man who picked him as a candidate, Evo Morales, was greeted by adoring crowds as he crossed into Bolivia from Argentina, a year after having to flee the country due to protests over electoral fraud. Still Luis Arce, having been Morales' Minister of Finance, insists that he is very much his own person. Many Bolivars believe, however, that his former boss is pulling the strings. In Colombia, Iván Duque was an inexperienced senator when he was elected to the top job in 2018, thanks to the backing of Álvaro Uribe, a conservative two-term former president who was barred from re-election by term limits. In Argentina, Cristina Fernández de Kirchner, president from 2007 to 2015, struck a deal with Alberto Fernández (no relation) whereby he ran and won in 2019, with her as his running mate. This proxy scheme is a great idea. Unfortunately, there have been times when it has gotten out of hand and the proxy, having smelled power, wants to be his or her own person, Brazil being a good example. Former President Luiz Inácio Lula da Silva (2003–2010) chose Dilma Rousseff to keep the presidential seat warm for him. But she outmaneuvered him to run for a second term, only to be unfairly impeached for breaking budget rules.

Beyond Term Limits

Once more, I'd like to reiterate that democracy fanatics have it all wrong when they suggest that term limits are good for a country. As I have been trying to explain, when a leader is popular, why force him or her out of the office? Most people like to know where they stand; they like stability. Maintaining the status quo is a very good thing. Continuous change has always been highly overrated. Isn't it nice when our children and grandchildren can look up to the same leader? It gives them someone permanent to identify with. And I'm sure that long-term continuity also must have its economic advantages. I believe that people have it all wrong when they associate these leaders for life with eras of stagnation—in other words, static economic, political, cultural, and social policies. For example, I always found it tragic that Leonid Brezhnev of the USSR got such a bad rap from people who had the nerve to criticize his long stay in power. It is really unfair to refer to this period in the history of Russia as "Brezhnevian Stagnation," suggesting that he was overly conservative in his running of the country, failing to change with the times. And it is unfair to suggest that his enlightened policies contributed to the breakup of the Soviet Union. It is even more unfair to listen to these false rumors that Putin, given his economic policies, is trying to imitate Brezhnev.

I really question whether it is also true that with term limits, leaders will be more pressured to deliver results, that they will be more motivated to leave their office with a positive legacy. I cannot help but seriously doubt whether the fact of having term limits will encourage a new generation of political leaders to come to the fore—to come up with fresh ideas and to embark on possible policy changes. In addition, I think people exaggerate when they say that in countries with leaders for life, there is a much greater probability for social unrest, and there will even be attempts at revolution. It is totally untrue that without term limits, rights abuses, secret or arbitrary arrests and detentions, tight restrictions on freedom of expression, and police brutality are more likely to occur. I also question, listening to these truly uninformed panicmongers, whether there is a greater chance for war under these leaders for life than with those leaders restricted by term limits. Some of these people come up with this crazy idea that leaders for life, when faced with waning popularity, may incite the population by inventing external threats. What these unfair critics also add is that such leaders will resort to these tactics to present themselves as the saviors of the nation. It is really unbelievable how low people can stoop to vilify these enlightened leaders who tend to have the best interests of their countries at heart. Everyone must know that leaders for life will always be defenders, not warmongers.

The Nepotistic, Kleptocratic Imperative

I also find it questionable when people suggest that with leaders for life, countries easily turn into nepotistic kleptocracies. People who make these negative comments are surely far off the mark. Of course, there is some truth in saying that leaders should pay attention to financial matters. But how wrong these critics are in saying—falsely, I should add—that many of these leaders only hang on to their position to have control over their country's resources. In a very derogatory way, they accuse them of kleptocratic practices. They even suggest, following this line of reasoning, that if these leaders would let go of their power base, they would not only lose their wealth, but potentially even face prosecution due to the way they have been handling their country's resources. If such a horrible situation were to transpire, they could even end up in prison—heaven forbid. Again, as far as I am concerned, people who make these slanderous remarks are far off the mark. It is beyond any reasonable doubt that these leaders for life, in dealing with financial matters, have the best interests of their countries at heart. In my opinion, idealistic as many of them tend to be, they merely like to distribute a country's resources in ways that benefit the smooth running of their countries.

Cultivating Nepotism and a Mafia-Like Inner Core

Furthermore, as far as nepotism is concerned, it strikes me that putting trusted people in key governmental positions is a no-brainer and another wise decision by these thoughtful leaders. To call this practice nepotism is nothing but a misnomer. On the contrary, to have the support of these people will help them to have a solid layer of oversight and control. Also, I should add that employing nepotism serves as a clever way of "coup-proofing" the country—limiting the possibility that some restless, uninformed souls will incite the population to rebel against their legitimate government.

But insightful as most of these leaders for life are, they realize the importance of funneling power to a small, some would even accusingly say mafia-like, inner core, made up of cronies, family, and tribal or ethnic interest. Delegating power to such a highly selected group of people will be helpful in protecting a leader from possible troublemakers. And since family members and friends are the closest to the leader, isn't it only natural to put them in charge of the security forces, both military and police? Sadly enough, often these leaders have no choice but to be watchful, as there will always be some rabble-rousers out there. At the same time (paranoia being the disease of kings), I find it also an excellent idea to have these very trusted people monitor each other. Isn't it a fantastic way to keep them on their toes? Unfortunately, in spite of these leaders' very good intentions, enemies can be everywhere.

Money Talks—Virtue of Paying People Off

Moreover, to ensure the loyalty of these people, it is important to incentivize them. After all, they deserve to be paid for their efforts in making their countries even greater. To even think of calling this kind of caring for their country corruption is far off the mark. I also believe that they shouldn't be the only ones to get paid. We all know that money talks. Financially supporting other potential allies—I have never liked the word "bribe"—has a very positive, creative influence. It is a much more enlightened way to help people out, as opposed to locking up, or murdering political rivals and other critics. Creating a codependency situation with the various constituencies that are important to a country, including the judiciary, has always come in handy. It cannot be said strongly enough how much these "creative" financial practices are needed to ensure stability—all are efforts in helping to make a country great.

Another example of envious people bad-mouthing enlightened practices is the accusation that the amassing of wealth by these leaders for life reduces most of the population to grinding poverty. It is incredible how low people will go in spreading false rumors. Take, for example, the case of former president José Eduardo dos Santos of Angola. I always thought that it was truly admirable that he made his daughter Isabel the wealthiest woman on the African continent. Wasn't he a true champion of affirmative action by making her also the chairperson of the country's national oil company? Given these great moves, it cannot but be slander to have some critics say that only the elites in the country have been reaping the benefits of the oil industry, while most Angolans are still living in arduous conditions indicated by the very high infant mortality rate, poor access to water and sanitation, and high degree of illiteracy.

Media and Culture Management

Naturally, it is also important that the members of the leader's inner circle monitor the media. There is nothing wrong with having these leaders for life be in full control of the flow of information. We all know that there is so much false information being spread around. Therefore, it makes good sense that they appoint people whose task it will be to prevent the population from getting the wrong ideas. Generally speaking, it will always be of utmost importance to have the media on their side. Of course, an important question that remains is how to deal with journalists who don't walk the line? What to do with the journalists that question a leader for life's good intentions? In some cases, I believe, harsh as it may sound, good riddance is the only answer. In that respect, Recep Tayyip Erdoğan, the president of Turkey, has been exemplary. He really knows how to deal with journalists. After a few of his "interventions," most of them, to the best of my knowledge, know what's good for them. And I have heard that Turkish prisons are not for everybody. That being said, it is very gratifying when most of the people in the media go out of their way to project an image of popular support and invulnerability toward their leaders. As things are presently, there is already far too much negative news being disseminated.

In addition, referring to the media, I think it is quite unfair when I hear complaints of the media's role in building cults of personality. In describing the many virtues of these leaders for life, again these people are just trying to contribute to their country's stability. They are doing nothing more than helping the general population understand what their leaders stand for. It makes for transparency. Thus, the creation of an ideology that summarizes the often-profound ideas of the leader is always going to be very useful. It is a great way to further legitimize the leader's position. I think, in this context, Turkmenbashi in using his seminal work *Ruhnama* has been a true role model. But to be frank, he followed a hallowed tradition of another great example, Mao Tse-tung's *Little Red Book*, from which President Xi Jinping learned and went on to introduce his own great *The Governance of China* bestseller trilogy. The same point can be made about the earlier mentioned *juche* concept of the Kim family in North Korea. Generally speaking, these ideologies are extremely enlightening when it comes to explaining why these leaders should occupy their position for life, and why their positions, if in any way possible, should be passed on to their descendants.

In Praise of Stability

I hope that by now I have made it quite clear that democracy in itself is an incredibly unstable system of government. By virtue of the way it has evolved, it will always be too much subjected to the whims and caprices of the general population. And as we have seen over and over again, people who advocate this form of government often ask for and sometimes demand changes that fundamentally undermine the smooth functioning of an administration. Furthermore, I should add that people who champion the idea of checks and balances—this strange notion of separation of powers to make leaders accountable—appear to live in la-la land. Having an independent judiciary, a free press, and other independent institutions only contributes to muddled governance. Too much consensus management doesn't make for a true focus. It only hampers decision-making. To insist on limitations to a leader's power will only limit his or her ability to govern well. Thus, I hope, in presenting this modest Swiftian-like proposal, I have made clear that democracies don't actually offer choice but rather the mere illusion of choice. Given the reality of the human condition, it is so much better not to beat around the bush, but instead to call a spade a spade as far as the realities of governing are concerned.

The reader must realize by now that I think that the idea of a government of the people, by the people, for the people is highly overrated. As I must have made quite clear, the common people most often don't know what they really want. Often, the best thing the silent majority can do is to take these words literally and to remain silent. Actually, staying silent might be in the best interest of everybody. After all, I have seen how all too often, democracies encourage the "infamous" majority to decide things about which it is quite ignorant. And as we can expect, it only leads to mediocracy. Thus, keeping this factor in mind, I once more pose the question of why we should have constitutional entrenchments of leadership terms. Why not just do away with it? Given how uninformed the general public tends to be, it is not in any country's interest to allow each citizen a voice in matters of state. All too often, it just leads to muddled governance.

Actually, isn't it true that in the final reckoning, it doesn't really matter whether a country is a democracy or an autocracy? What really matters is the quality of its leadership. And isn't it correct to assume that the longer these leaders are in power, the more experience they will acquire in governing? It makes my plea for having more leaders for life self-explanatory. I strongly believe that the countries that take this option are the ones that will really succeed, as it makes for political and policy continuity. All of us know that consistency and continuity are the building blocks that create trust.

The doubters of this form of governance better keep in mind that trust isn't built by having a revolving door of ever-changing leaders, as tends to be the case in these so-called liberal democracies. These democratic fantasies are only prescriptions for confusion, conflict, and social unrest. And as we have seen over and over again, most often, these supposedly democratic politicians tend to be totally overrated. We find too many "post turtles" among them. Therefore, given how muddled their actions often tend to be, it is obviously so much better to have a strongman leader rather than having to deal with the often corrupt, political, democratic establishment. That some of them may have a few narcissistic quirks is just par for the course. Obviously, they behave the way they do because they know what is in the best interest of their countries.

Democracy—Worst Form of Government, Except for All the Others

My hope is that more leaders from around the world are prepared to tell their voters that a regular change of leadership is a terrible idea. Instead, they should tell them that having leaders for life is really the way to go forward. In clarifying their position, they should also make quite clear that democracy is not the answer to having well-oiled governance. It should be seen as another form of opium for the people. It just creates pleasant illusions.

In this context, I remember what Winston Churchill once said: "The best argument against democracy is a five-minute talk with the average voter." This observation can't be more to the point. I hate to admit, however, that what confused me was that he also added: "Democracy is the worst form of government, except for all the others." I am still wondering what he really meant by those words. What has puzzled me even more has been hearing other people say that democracy is not just the right to have a voice, but most importantly, it is the right to live a life of dignity. Given these words, I have to admit that, in some of my darker moments, I find myself asking whether there might be something wrong with this idea of having leaders for life. Could it even be that everything about it is wrong? Is it possible that I'm wrong? Perhaps, however, the following fairy tale will provide some clarity about the right course for us to take. Also, it may point out to us what may go wrong!

3

The Little Drum Boy or the Rise and Fall of a Flawed Leader

Where there is much pride or much vanity, there will also be much revengefulness.
—Arthur Schopenhauer

The lion is most handsome when looking for food.
—Rumi

Once Upon a Time

Once upon a time, in a land far, far away, when kings still ruled the Earth, there lived a hard man named Old Drum, who had five children. In spite of his many children, however, only one son became the apple of his eye. The other children didn't give him much pleasure. But the son who was singled out was looked at by his father as the person who would make the Drum name live on in perpetuity.

Now, reflecting on this opening, I wonder whether this is the best way to start this tale of woe. Perhaps I should have started it differently, making clear at the onset that, as this fairy tale runs its course, both wonderful and terrible events will transpire. That's the reason this tale can be called a fairy tale. After all, as I have said in the introduction of this book of essays, fairy tales help us to understand what's really important to us. They amuse and entertain; they also bring comfort and consolation. Furthermore, they give us hope that somehow, we can be saved, rescued, and healed. That's the reason why fairy tales have retained their popularity. And even though fairy tales take place in magical kingdoms that are far, far away, these stories can also teach us important lessons about life that are still relevant in our day and age. They tell us something profound and essential—namely, that while the world we live in can be dark and scary, and even full of monsters, it is possible for these monsters to be slain.

Having made these opening statements, let me start again, as I'm not sure what kind of perpetuity Old Drum had in mind. Did he want the name Drum to become famous or famously infamous? Also, before I take up the thread of this story once more, with fairy tales isn't there always the question of whether the story really happened or whether what we experienced was just a pipe dream? I'm making these comments because so much of what will be told may sound so strange that it doesn't make much sense. But whether it actually makes sense or not, the time is long past to think about these matters, as much of this story's history has been lost in time. Actually, some people even questioned whether this tragic tale ever did take place. They very much prefer to forget whatever happened. It was just too much of a dark page in the history of the country. Thus, taking these musings into consideration, let's once more start this tale of woe—the rise and fall of a king in a land far, far away.

Once upon a time, when the world was still young, in a land that's not unfamiliar to many of us, there lived a very ambitious man named Old Drum—the name "Drum" derived from the German word "Trommel," which was the origin of the surname "Trump." But people in the know thought that this name described him quite well, given all the "drumming" that he did. Everybody who met him noted that, with him around, there was this constant, irritating, rhythmic noise. Old Drum had the habit of repeating the same messages over and over again, as if he was afraid that people weren't really listening to what he had to say. Actually, he might have been right in thinking that his egocentric "dialogues" were meeting with a poor reception.

If the truth be told, many of the people who came to know Old Drum somewhat better would close their ears. They experienced it as quite tiring to listen to his long harangues—to all his drumming. His stories were just too monotonous. What didn't help was that these stories would always be about him. He wasn't interested in listening to other people's tales. As a matter of fact, Old Drum could be described as a terrible listener. He seemed to be so completely caught up in his own world that he paid no attention whatsoever to what other people had to say. Instead, he would go on and on talking about anything that came into his mind. And his harangues always had to do with what he believed was wrong with the world, and how he—if he only had the power—would set the world straight.

Apart from Old Drum's wish to create a world that was more to his liking, his harangues also included stories about the many great things that he was doing. Most people, however, found it extremely tiresome to hear again and again how successful he was, how much money he was making, and the creative tricks he used to avoid paying his taxes. Clearly, Old Drum was very proud of his material successes. The amount of money he earned and his self-esteem seemed to be closely related. What also became quite clear in hearing his stories was that lying and cheating were part and parcel of his method for becoming such a financial success. Perhaps, the French novelist Honoré de Balzac had a point when he said that "behind every great fortune is an equally great crime." Old Drum, however, would present these semilegal maneuvers of how to increase his wealth as very legitimate business practices. But for most people his rantings about the wrongs of the world and his wealth became quite tiresome. They wanted to have nothing to do with him. No wonder that Old Drum felt misunderstood.

When Old Drum began to realize that most people didn't pay attention to his words of wisdom, he asked himself what he could do to be truly noticed. What would get everyone's attention? How could he make the name Drum famous all over the land?

Initially, Old Drum was quite at a loss as to how to go about it. But he had always taken to heart the statement by Emperor Napoleon Bonaparte: "Glory is fleeting but obscurity is forever." Heaven forbid the Drum name would fall into obscurity, he thought. It would be a fate worse than death. That needed to be prevented at all costs. This thought increased his determination to have the family name written into the history books.

The Quest

After thinking more about the matter, Old Drum had a Eureka moment. Of course, he thought, he had to create a dynasty if he wanted to put the family name into the history books. Clearly, merely being rich was not good enough. As he was learning the hard way given all the people who were avoiding him, money alone wouldn't be sufficient. Much more was needed to be respected all over the land. But giving the matter some more thought, he realized if he really wanted to make the family name famous, he needed help. It wasn't a task that could be easily undertaken alone. He had come to realize that he possessed neither the charm nor the charisma necessary to have people pay attention.

Old Drum concluded that the best way to go about making his name famous was by having children. Children would be the ideal way to build a dynasty. And the more he thought about it, children could complement him. They could help do the things he wasn't really good at. And, as he told himself, as they were quite malleable when young, he could shape them according to his own image. Furthermore, there was yet another thought that gave him much comfort, after he would have indoctrinated them, they could become his emissaries in his quest for fame.

Truth be told, Old Drum had as of yet no children, the implication being that he needed to find a woman—a person who was prepared to help him in his quest. Given his many quirks, however, finding a woman was easier said than done. Old Drum wasn't the most agreeable person to live with. In spite of his wealth, all of the women he had approached in the past had refused his offer of marriage. What made them reluctant to commit themselves was that they were repelled by his self-centeredness, monomaniacal interest in money, and his lack of emotional responsiveness. Therefore, given Old Drum's personality makeup, it was quite fortunate that after a long search he found a woman ready to serve his purpose. Unsophisticated as she was—as a poor immigrant not having a penny to her name—financial security was a very high priority to her. That made her exactly the kind of person Old Drum was looking for. She would suit his purpose very well. And, fortunately, what also proved to be fortuitous was that she turned out to be very fertile, bearing him five children.

Although Old Drum now had many children who could help him create a dynasty, sadly enough, only one found favor in his eyes. Most of them, he was quick to say, he considered as totally unsuitable to help him in his quest. For example, due to bad luck (to use Old Drum's own words), two turned out to be girls. As a misogynist, he discounted them immediately. Furthermore, to his great disappointment, his youngest son also proved to be quite useless. As the baby of the family, he was spoiled terribly by his wife. According to Old Drum, he would never be tough enough to help him in his quest. And if that wasn't the only setback, the oldest son on whom Old Drum had placed high hopes also turned out to be a weakling. Not that Old Drum hadn't tried to toughen him up, but whatever heroic efforts he had made, he was unable to make a real "man" out of him. He couldn't pass Old Drum's tests of character. If Old Drum was to be believed, this son would never be the "killer" he wanted him to be. He was just too soft. And since any sign of softness was unthinkable to Old Drum, the oldest son was also cast aside. Sadly enough, he would become the black sheep of the family.

But the failure of the oldest son to live up to Old Drum's high standards offered an opportunity for his second son, whom he had baptized Drum Jr. This son, having looked at the scary interchanges between his father and his older brother, decided that showing any sign of weakness would be a great mistake. It would only make him the butt of his father's wrath. No wonder that he made up his mind to never become like his eldest brother. Becoming the black sheep of the family was not for him. Heaven forbid, he thought, "I don't want to be screamed at in public. I don't want to be told that I am an idiot!" In order to please his father, Drum Jr. told himself: "I never should admit to mistakes. It is much better to lie or blame others." Thus, he realized from early on that taking personal responsibility when something went wrong would be a great mistake. The only thing that would come out of it was making his father mad.

While Drum Jr. was learning these lessons, life for his eldest brother was rapidly spinning out of control. Predictably, given all the pressure his father was putting on him, it was coming to a bad end. Old Drum's dire predictions had turned into a self-fulfilling prophecy. Unable to find favor in his father's eyes, the eldest son sought relief in alcohol, an addiction that eventually would contribute to his premature death. No wonder that Old Drum would focus all his attention onto his second son. Given his obsession about the quest, Drum Jr. became the only person that would really matter in the Drum family.

Pugna Ego Cogito Ergo Sum: I Fight Therefore I Am

To continue this tale of woe about the making of a king, Old Drum's wife became sick and depressed after the birth of her fifth child. Given her feeble mental state, the sad outcome of her illness was that Drum Jr. would see very little of his mother. Whatever efforts he made at getting her attention, she was unavailable to cater to his needs. Whatever care she could offer, it was always focused on her newborn. Predictably, her emotional absence created in Drum Jr. the feeling of not being loved. And sadly enough, if truth be told, her unavailability would scar him for life. What didn't help was his mother's own neediness. Frequently, it seemed as if she wanted her children to take care of her, not the other way around. And as she had to deal with a very demanding, but emotionally absent husband, she came to present herself as the martyr of the household.

A Father's Education

As time went by, whatever caretaking the children needed, that task was handed over to a number of ever-changing servants. In the meantime, in Drum Jr.'s imagination, his mother had turned into something of a "ghost"—a mysterious female apparition that would not play an active role in the records of his life. In contrast to his wife, however, Old Drum was very much present, but not in a caring capacity. While at an emotional level his wife was very needy, any emotional expressiveness on his side was completely absent, exacerbating the prevailing, extremely dysfunctional family dynamics. Old Drum was present, however, in another, much harsher capacity. After having crushed his eldest son psychologically with his bullying, he was now giving his full attention to Young Drum. And even though he didn't say so explicitly, he wanted this son—whatever it would take—to become an extension of himself. This son was the one to be anointed to fulfill his quest; this son was the one to be sent on a mission. To Old Drum, Drum Jr. was his last hope in making the family name famous—to have the family name written into the history books.

Old Drum would be telling himself how extraordinary Drum Jr. really was. At the same time, he would ignore and rationalize his son's many shortcomings. To acknowledge that his chosen successor possessed weaknesses had become unimaginable. It would be too painful to contemplate. Again and again, Old Drum would convince himself that his second son was the answer to all his problems; that he would be the one that would help him succeed in his quest for fame.

Sadly enough, however, Old Drum's strange ways of attending to this son created the foundation for Drum Jr.'s deep, underlying insecurity. It prevented him from developing as a complete, well-rounded human being. It made it impossible for him to become a person in his own right—to acquire an identity of his own. Instead, Drum Jr. always felt compelled to wear some kind of mask. As his father appeared to him larger than life, he seemed to have no choice but to be an extension of him.

There were times, however, given the kind of "overstimulation" Drum Jr. was exposed to, when he wondered whether he really deserved all of his father's attention. Would he ever be able to live up to these expectations? Was it all real? Or was it just fake? Therefore, to find some kind of emotional balance, the only alternative left open to him was to rationalize whatever unrealistic expectations his father had put on him. But as time went by, Drum Jr. began to believe his own press. Unfortunately, given the cues he received from his father, he was becoming a man of borrowed qualities.

3 The Little Drum Boy or the Rise and Fall of a Flawed Leader

In spite of the exaggerated expectations placed on his son, Old Drum did realize that the journey to train Drum Jr. for the task at hand was going to be a difficult one. It would take a lot of hard work to toughen him up. But it wouldn't be impossible. He only needed "to drum" into his son the things that he felt were important. In particular, as part of his unusual educational program, Old Drum would tell his son over and over again: "You have to become number one; you have to be a killer."

What being a killer meant to Old Drum was having his son win at all costs. At the same time, the hidden agenda was (even though it was not so hidden) whenever things went wrong (which was often) he should deny any form of responsibility. Like his father had been doing all his life, he should learn to transfer blame to others. He should never show any sign of weakness. To be a loser was unimaginable. Clearly, what was of utmost importance to Old Drum was to create a son who was ruthless. But as we have learned from other fairy tales, telling a child something is one thing, but making it happen is a very different matter altogether. It may lead to quite unexpected outcomes.

In spite of what Old Drum was up against, he was a persistent educator. What we have learned about him is that he wasn't the kind of person who would easily give up. And certainly he wasn't giving up on Young Drum, this son being his last hope. It made him unstoppable when it came to turn this son into a fighter. Whatever the price, he was to become the puppeteer of his son's life. As Old Drum would tell himself, only by having him pull the strings could he make his son ruthless. It was really up to him to teach Drum Jr. that in the world they were living, there was no place for compassion, empathy, generosity, integrity, and responsibility. His son needed to know in no uncertain terms that emotional sensitivity was for the birds. At all costs, his son needed to become tough and resilient. And if in molding him in this way, he would be interfering with his son's ability to experience the entire spectrum of human emotions, so be it. Old Drum strongly believed that his son should never be dependent on other people—a principle he applied to himself as well. Heaven forbid he should turn into a weakling like all the other children. Instead, he should become a fighter. He had to become the person etching the Drum name into the history books. This son had to make it happen.

To toughen up Drum Jr. even more, his father would tell him repeatedly that the world was a dangerous place—that "it was a jungle with winners and losers." And within this jungle, as he repeatedly pointed out, humans are the most vicious of all animals, thus making clear to his son that he should always be on his guard. If not, according to Old Drum, the jungle would chew him up and spit him out. At the same time, he assured Drum Jr. that if he would become tough and mean enough, he could hit it big—really big.

In a way, Old Drum had made it big. By hook and by crook, he had made his fortune in the property business. Making money had always come naturally to him, a talent he had liked Drum Jr. also to acquire. And in emphasizing the importance of making money, he would always point out to him that money was an ideal way to keep score—to show who was the top dog. To make his son realize the value of money—seeing it as an excellent way of toughening him up—Old Drum often took him along to collect outstanding debts. Once, on one of these trips, Drum Jr. asked his father why he always stood to the side of the debtor's door after ringing the bell. "Because sometimes they shoot right through the door" was his father's response. It was the kind of lesson Drum Jr. never forgot. Once more, it made him realize he would need to be vigilant and fierce if he were to survive in the world he lived in.

At times, when Old Drum was in a relaxed, friendly mood, he would even whisper to his son that he had all that it took to become a king. It was the kind of whispering that Drum Jr. really liked. At the same time, his father would tell him over and over again that if he wanted to go for that prize, he really had to be a killer. He certainly needed to be ruthless. He would need to take risks. And to be able to get his way, he might even have to go over dead bodies. Clearly, to Old Drum, principles were for others, an observation that very much began to resonate with his son. At the same time, Drum Jr. was also very aware of the fact that not following his father's admonitions (his eldest brother being the dreaded negative example) could only lead to severe, even public humiliation.

The Making of a Man Without Qualities

Sadly enough, given the indoctrination given to him by his father, Drum Jr. became a rather lonely, psychologically very damaged young man. Some psychologists would later note that his father had perverted his son's perception of the world, hampering the prospect of being well adjusted. As his father had planned, Drum Jr. was becoming an extension of Old Drum, not a person in his own right. And the way this development took place meant that he never would possess a stable, inner core. Thus, given the strange role his father played in his life, whatever little self-confidence he possessed, it would always need constant reinforcement. Thus, due to the strange family dynamics that he was exposed to, Drum Jr. was left with a very fragile ego, always feeling like an impostor. And given his intense sense of insecurity, he would always ask himself whether other people could see through his bravura. Whatever efforts

Young Drum would make to project an aura of self-confidence, it would never be more than a façade.

Given what had happened within the family, at all times, Drum Jr. would tell himself that he was so much better than his eldest brother, that he would never be like him. Instead, he would repeat to himself that he was the smartest, the greatest, the most talented person who walked about. And as he had to be his own cheerleader, he said it so often that he ended up believing his own stories. In spite of having internalized his own hype, deep down he knew that whatever success he had in life, it was very much because of his father's money and power. He also knew, whenever he would be in trouble, he could always count on his father to bail him out. Although he would pretend that this wasn't the case, Drum Jr. had been provided with an incredible safety net. In his darker moments, however—taking a hard look at himself—he knew that he had never really accomplished anything of substance by himself. Thus, sadly enough, due to his father's unusual education, Drum Jr. didn't have the opportunity to really grow up. Realistically speaking, he remained stuck at an infantile stage, not able to further learn, grow, or evolve.

Given his many insecurities, the world Drum Jr. had created for himself was perceived as a very dangerous place. It would be a place where he always had to be on guard. Never would he forget his father's admonitions about it being a jungle out there; never would he forget that he lived in a world where he believed that everyone was out to get him. Throughout his whole life, he would strongly believe that life consisted of a series of battles during which there were winners and losers. And, heaven forbid, he could never allow himself to be a loser. He needed to win at all costs. If he would lose, the humiliation would just be too excruciating. No wonder that he always felt he had to appear strong, even though it was all fake. No wonder that he always needed to put on a mask. No wonder that he never could show any sign of vulnerability. His insecurities also explained why coming close to people was always seen as fraught with danger. If other people would understand how insecure he really was—that inside of him there was very little substance—he was sure that he would be taken advantage of.

The Basic Psychological Architecture

Fortunately, many of Old Drum's lessons in toughness dovetailed with Drum Jr.'s very aggressive temperament. Thus, as could be predicted, given his father's unusual educational program, Drum Jr. transformed into the most confrontational kid in the neighborhood. Having internalized his father's lessons on how to become a bully, he turned into one himself. He made it very clear that nobody should dare to stand in his way. And the people who would dare to do so, quickly realized that they were doing so at their own peril. A rebuke by anyone was seen as a challenge that required instant retaliation, preferably a very aggressive one. And if revenge was involved, they could always expect the worst. The way Drum Jr.'s father had "programmed" his son, acting differently was impossible.

As the years went by, Drum Jr. acquired a reputation of being an especially unruly kid. He became well known for his talent in terrorizing the other children in the neighborhood. Whenever he saw an opportunity, he would use his fists to assert his authority, taking great pleasure out of the many fights he got himself into. But it was also like each of these transgressions was a show put on for his father to demonstrate how tough he really was.

Given this dysfunctional developmental trajectory, it became increasingly difficult to deal with Young Drum. What made it even more difficult was his behavior at school, where he was an extremely poor student. He lacked the intellectual curiosity to explore new things. Dealing with cognitive complexity—that is, the mental processes needed to derive new information out of given information with the intention of solving problems, making decisions, and planning actions—was far beyond him. And if that wasn't enough of a handicap, open-mindedness was also not part of his makeup. Learning new things was not really for him. Instead, constantly bored with what his teachers had to say, Drum Jr. would act out violently in class, making his teachers angry. It was such behavior that led to detention after detention. Once, he even punched his music teacher, giving the woman a black eye.

The Finishing Touches

Although Old Drum did appreciate these signs of toughness in his son, continuing to encourage him to be a "killer," he wasn't keen about the prospect of turning him into a juvenile delinquent. Therefore, in his father's eyes, Drum Jr. went one step too far when he was kicked out of school after having threatened some people with a pair of switchblades. To prevent his son from truly turning into a hooligan, Old Drum decided to dispatch him to a military academy. He strongly believed that he needed to alloy his son's aggression with a modicum of harsh discipline.

To everyone's surprise, Drum Jr. very much liked life at the military academy, one explanation being that kindness and compassion was not part of the school's educational curriculum. For the streetfighter that he had become, the academy turned out to be a perfect home. Drum Jr. found it enjoyable to be part of an aggressive and isolated subculture that prized physical toughness and that defined manhood in its basest terms. He liked being part of a world where a pseudo-military type of hierarchical behavior prevailed. He liked living in a place run by rough, ex-military drill sergeants who would beat the hell out of him if he disobeyed their orders.

Moreover, he liked the fact that the military academy was very much a man's world—a place where women were almost nonexistent. Like his mother had been absent in his life, at the academy, women were also absent—something that very much resonated with Young Drum, as he was quite uncomfortable with women. Actually, the only female role models the students in the academy would pay some attention to were the ones that appeared in the pages of Playboy. Drum Jr. had entered a world where women were seen as "part objects" to be considered only for sexual purposes.

Generally speaking, it can be said that the military academy became Drum Jr.'s finishing school. It transformed him into the person he would end up being. Similar to the lessons drummed into him by his father, it would teach him once more that life was all about the survival of the fittest, that the world was truly Darwinian. It taught him that the only way to survive in this world was to fight aggression with aggression. No wonder he appreciated the academy that had the kind of aggressive ambiance where fighting was appreciated.

As we have seen, fighting had always energized Young Drum. Fighting made him feel most alive. And as time went by, the need to quarrel over even the smallest things had become a fundamental existential need. Drum Jr. would even create fights when he felt that things were too peaceful. While for others the mantra would have been "I think, thus I am," for Drum Jr. it had morphed into "I fight, thus I am." He had learned the value of turning the passive into the active. Instead of waiting for things to happen, he would make it happen. Throughout his life, "protective retaliation"—lashing out at people he viewed as potential adversaries—would always be his rallying cry.

In more than one way, Drum Jr.'s stay at military school can be considered as an educational success of some sort. It prevented him from turning into a real thug. It taught him the importance of appearances—to pretend that, at times, it was advisable to behave in somewhat more diplomatic ways. And it taught him a modicum, but only a modicum, of impulse control. It was a place where he learned how to present a veneer of civility, how to manage his explosive aggressivity. Still, there were many occasions when Drum Jr. wouldn't be able to control himself—when he would resort to rather impulsive, seemingly irrational behavior and actions. Of course, as many psychologists would suggest much later, there was always a rationale behind these strange outbursts. All in all, the military school transformed Drum Jr. into a highly competitive, but insecure, young man in a highly competitive environment.

Later in life, looking back at his stay at the military school, Drum Jr. always expressed great satisfaction with the experience. If truth be told, he would repeatedly say it was the academy that made a real man out of him. And if people would press him to elaborate, he would state how he liked the male chauvinistic atmosphere, how he liked the hierarchical structure, how he liked the uniforms, how he liked the drills, and how he liked the pageantry of the parades—a love he shared with his mother, who would always become very agitated seeing the pageantry of royalty and coronations. No wonder that Drum Jr. would later become the ultimate showman, citing as his inspiration his mother's love of the dramatic and the grand.

Also, as was to be expected given his mindset, during Drum Jr.'s stay at the military academy, he never had any close confidants. His competitiveness, his need for attention, adulation, and affirmation had crowded out any possibility of real friendships. Given his mantra of needing to be tough, it would be impossible for Drum Jr. to show the kind of vulnerability that the true intimacy of real friendships typically requires. To form real attachments—to come close to people—was far too threatening.

It could very well be that Drum Jr. was afraid that, if he would come too close to people, they might see through him. And, heaven forbid, they might even guess that under this veneer of toughness was hovering an incredible amount of vulnerability. Who knows, they might even make fun of him, realizing that much of his behavior was merely a highly dramatic performance to impress others. To look into himself, to find out what he was all about, would never be for him. It would just be too scary. And as Drum Jr. would state quite bluntly much later, any form of psychological introspection is only for weaklings. In reality, he may have been afraid that it would have exposed him as a fake, that others would realize that behind all his aggressive, self-confident posturing, there was really very little to show, that his growing arrogance was just a protective cover for his many insecurities.

Given his delicate psychological equilibrium, what would always be of utmost importance to Drum Jr., however, was to be noticed. No wonder that as time passed he increasingly became a master of self-promotion and hyperbole. He would do anything to get people's attention, happily resorting to exaggeration and lies—a pattern he had learned early in life. Another way to have people notice—perfected during his stay at the military academy—was to demean anybody that would stand in his way. Old Drum's son had become a master in handing out denigrating nicknames. The art of humiliation was part of his repertoire—Old Drum being a great role model. He hadn't forgotten how expertly his father had humiliated his elder brother.

Feeling Alone While Playing to the Crowd

Generally speaking, Old Drum was quite pleased that his son now possessed the kind of aggressive discipline that he always wanted him to have. He was no longer worried about Drum Jr.'s uncontrolled aggression. He was no longer fearful that it would end up in disaster. As things were panning out, he had created the foundation for enabling his son to make his mark in the world.

As Old Drum told himself, while he didn't possess the talent to capture the attention of people, it was there for all to see that his son was quite different. Drum Jr. had acquired the qualities needed to be a showman. Old Drum very much admired his son's ease in relating to others. As he had planned, Drum Jr. would be the public face for his thwarted ambition. As things were now, his success and that of his son were intricately linked. Old Drum told himself that his son was getting ready for the quest.

Also, what very much pleased Old Drum was that his son had been accepted into one of the better universities in the country. What he didn't know—although he might even have been proud of his son's ingenuity—was that Drum Jr. had paid somebody else to take the entrance exam. Drum Jr. strongly believed that it was the thing to do, as his grade point average—which put him far from the top of his class—would have prevented him from getting into this university. Later on, he would boast about his admittance to the place, saying it made him truly a very balanced, super genius. Again, for Drum Jr., cheating and lying—while deceiving himself—had become an ingrained, defensive behavior pattern. It had always been the way to circumvent his father's disapproval, the way to avoid punishment. Principles were for others, but not for him.

Clearly, given the education that Drum Jr. received while growing up, he would, whenever he saw an opportunity, pull a fast one on anyone who stood in his way. Whenever the situation allowed it, he would try to take advantage of the other. As had been hammered into him, he always needed to win. And as he believed that it was a dog-eat-dog world where nobody could be trusted (parroting his father's own words), it was the right way to go about things. It was yet another reason why Drum Jr. was never able to make real friends at school. And it also explained why he had no real friends later in life. Whatever pseudo friendships he had as an adult, they would always be of an opportunistic nature and quite fleeting. He had learned the lesson quite well that any real emotional attachment needed to be avoided at all costs. Trusting anyone, including his many wives, would always be fraught with danger. Real intimacy and care would never be for him. As mentioned before, his wives too were considered merely as sexual objects. Otherwise, it was wise to stay away from them. They would just make him feel uncomfortable. Unfortunately, having such an outlook to life made Drum Jr. an extremely lonely person.

As this fairy tale makes quite clear, Drum Jr., in turning into the proxy in his father's quest to create a dynasty, never possessed the psychological architecture that would enable him to build deep relationships with other people. And, sadly enough, he never even experienced the desire to do so. In that respect, he very much had some of the characteristics of what psychologists would call the avoidant personality. But that wasn't all. Narcissistic and psychopathic features were also not strange to him. These qualities were an important part of his personality makeup. This didn't make for a very attractive human "package." But as things stood now, what mattered was only to make the Drum name famous, everything else be damned. And to make this quest a reality, nobody should have the nerve to stand in his way.

Again, it explained Drum Jr.'s conviction that any real attachment would only complicate what he was striving for. Real attachment would only create indebtedness. As was visible for all to see, the only attachment he ever really cared about was himself. From a young age onward, given his insecurities, what would always be of overriding importance was having others acknowledge him, cheer him on telling him how great he was, and have others fill the emptiness that he felt inside. But in spite of his many insecurities, he would never demonstrate an inkling of self-doubt. On the contrary, his behavior would always be just the opposite. He would brag about his achievements in business (even though his father had to bail him out time after time when things went wrong). Also, throughout his life (in that respect being very much his father's son), he would always see other people in monetary terms, to be slotted as financial winners and losers.

In addition, for Drum Jr., cheating would always be a way of life. Hard, honest work was never expected of him. Instead, he would brag about his important contacts (although most people tried to avoid him). He would brag about his sexual relations (fleeting as they always tended to be). What truthfully could be said about him, however, was that there were failed business ventures, broken marriages, and a complete lack of true friends. Later, when Drum Jr. became king, his incapacity to act selflessly toward others—his inability to connect truly emotionally with his constituency—should be seen as another reflection of his inner emptiness. Emotional expressiveness would never be part of his psychological makeup.

At the same time, Drum Jr. had also developed a repertoire of skills Old Drum didn't possess. As mentioned before, he had turned into a high priest of self-promotion. He had become a great marketeer. He even managed to create the illusion—through a book he had written by using the writing skills of someone else—that he was a master dealmaker. These were the kind of things that Old Drum's money alone had never been able to buy. In that respect, father and son had become quite complementary. Thus, while his son played to the crowd up front—being a master in grandstanding—his father was in charge of the back office. In more than one way, Old Drum was now able to live vicariously through his son. Given his son's importance in his quest toward fame, he would always be there, prepared to protect him from his many disastrous business adventures.

We may wonder whether Old Drum ever realized the delicate psychological equilibrium of his son. Sadly enough, as he has passed away, we will never know. What we do know is that given Drum Jr.'s endless business failures, his ego needed to be bolstered continuously because he knew, deep down, that he wasn't at all what he pretended to be. But whatever his handicaps, he seemed to manage. As a master illusionist, he had learned how to pretend. He knew how to externalize his mishaps. Whatever misadventures occurred, they would always be the fault of others, as Drum Jr. needed to maintain his delusional belief about his brilliance and superiority. In reality, however, instead of trying to delude himself of being a successful, self-made entrepreneur, he was merely a rich, very spoiled playboy.

A Damaged Leader's Character Armor

To continue this unusual fairy tale, it was fortunate that Young Drum's strange upbringing endowed him with a number of qualities that would serve him quite well when he made a late-career entry as king. But as many were eager to point out, a philosopher-king he never would be. To be of service to others was not going to be part of Drum Jr.'s DNA. For this deeply damaged person, servant leadership would never be an option. Instead, what would always be of overriding importance to him was looking out for number one. And, as said before, given his feelings of inner emptiness, Drum Jr. would always need a constant stream of attention, adulation, and affirmation. Fortunately, satisfying these needs very much dovetailed with his father's wish to make the Drum name famous.

Looking Out for Number One

Given the way he was shaped psychologically, Drum Jr. became the kind of leader who would say: when the going gets tough, the buck stops with everybody—everybody else but never with him. When faced with failure, he knew how to deflect attention from himself. He knew how to create distractions. He knew how to create alternative realities, distorting what had really happened. When necessary, he would go in all directions to obfuscate whatever went wrong in his business dealings. It would always be the fault of the others: the economy, the banks, competitors, or just bad luck. To take personal responsibility for a mishap would never come to mind. What must be clear by now is that Drum Jr. had fine-tuned the art of always blaming others when things didn't turn out as expected. At the same time, you could count on him to be the first to take credit when things would turn out right.

Drum Jr.'s educational trajectory had turned him into not only a flaming narcissist, but a narcissist of the malignant type, given the vindictive side of his character. It implies a dark blend of narcissism and psychopathy, the latter characteristic (as described by psychiatrists and psychoanalysts) turning him also into an antisocial personality.[1] People acquainted with him would comment that his ego had become insatiable. Whatever the dialogue, it would be about Young Drum. He always needed to be the center of attention. It seemed like this emptiness inside him—this feeling of never feeling good enough—needed to be filled constantly. But whatever positive feedback was given, it was never sufficient.

All his life, Drum Jr. was hampered by this lack of adjustment between his psychobiological needs and the care that had been provided to him—by the fact that both parents had been absent, emotionally. Also, as has been noted, a close, loving relationship with his mother had never materialized. What worsened the situation was his father's use of his son as an extension of himself—his desire to make Drum Jr. his replica. But while trying to create his son in his own image, he had always put excessively high expectations on him, making him never feel good enough. And while all this pressure was put on him, Drum Jr. was never given the nurturance he craved for. Whatever his own needs were, they never mattered. At the same time, Drum Jr. knew that he had no choice. What he had realized soon enough was that if he wouldn't follow his father's wishes, he would be emotionally crushed, like what had happened to his brother. Thus, he had no option but to become the extension

---

[1] Manfred F. R. Kets de Vries (2019). *Down the Rabbit Hole of Leadership: Leadership Pathology in Everyday Life*. London: Palgrave Macmillan.

of his father. It left him, however, without a stable inner core. No wonder that he had become so unbalanced, psychologically. No wonder that he possessed such an unstable self-image, needing constant reinforcement.

Ironically, to continue this tale of woe, Drum Jr.'s lack of real attention from his parents resulted in a great need for attention. At the same time, his inner insecurity became his driving force to make something of himself, just as his father had planned. Thus, Drum Jr.'s compulsion to be noticed explained his rather bombastic way of dealing with whoever crossed his path. It also explained his desperate need to pursue positive emotional experiences, whether they would come in the form of social approval, fame, or wealth. Over time, all too well, he had incorporated the lessons learned from his father: it is better to be famous than to be forgotten. Old Drum's admonitions about the importance of the family name would always be at the top of his mind.

Later, when Drum Jr. became a property developer like his father, he would pick up on any chance to put the family name on his buildings. Unlike his father, however, he didn't turn into gold whatever he touched. Most often, his ventures turned into dismal failures, a fact that he could easily ignore as his father would always bail him out. And frankly speaking, at this stage of life, Old Drum didn't have much of a choice. His destiny had become very much tied up with his incompetent son. He was forced to protect Drum Jr. from his many foibles. And one way of managing this process was to surround him with people who could help him navigate and cover his tracks in the far more complex wider world. They would try to normalize his often rather strange, impulsive actions. In addition, these "minders" would lie for him, giving him credit for things he hadn't done—thus giving him a false sense of accomplishment. They would also go to great lengths to prop up his image of a bold, brash, self-made dealmaker. In reality, however, as must have been clear to the reader by now, Drum Jr. was mostly an abject failure, who in spite of all his cheating was incapable of achieving much on his own merits. Whatever he did, it turned out to be one spectacular failure after another. Whatever money Old Drum threw at him, it led to even riskier ventures, and even more dramatic failures.

But although Drum Jr. was not at all what he claimed to be, encouraged by his father, he believed his own hype. And, while his father would be described by his other children as being "tighter than a duck's ass," he would always behave quite differently with Drum Jr. With respect to this son, he was always prepared to waste significant amounts of money to cover his losses. To face reality, to accept the fraud his son really was had become unacceptable. He had to prop up the Frankenstein monster that he had created. Gradually, through these kinds of mental acrobatics, father and son appeared to be part of a *folie à deux*. Old Drum would boast about his son's greatness, and, for all to see, his delusional aggrandizements.

As we are learning from this fairy tale, Old Drum had successfully created a malignant narcissistic, damaged man. What was there for all to see was a person who was ignorant, incapable, completely out of his depth, but stuck in a delusional spin about his own greatness. All in all, Drum Jr. would always be totally unprepared to solve the problems that he would create for himself. He would be everything but what he pretended to be. Instead of being a successful businessman, he had built a reputation for himself for bad investments given his extremely poor judgments. And when things went wrong—which was often the case—he was also known for not honoring his promises, actions that wouldn't bother him at all. Having a guilty conscience was never part of his psychological makeup, highlighting his psychopathic qualities.

The Autocratic Imperative

Drum Jr.'s stay at the military academy had also been the finishing school for his love for authoritarianism. He always liked the slogan "my way or the highway." He liked to give orders. Consulting others was not really his forte. Command and control had always been more to his liking. Ironically, given his history as a troublemaker, law and order would also be one of his slogans. Of course, what helped him in being attracted toward a more autocratic leadership style was the domineering role model provided by his father. In that respect, he had very much become his father's son.

Accordingly, Drum Jr.'s rather rigid outlook toward the world gave him a set of attitudes and values that revolved around adherence to society's conventional norms, submission to the authorities who would personify or reinforce those norms, and an antipathy—to the point of hatred and aggression— toward those who would either challenge in-group norms or lie outside his self-created orbit. In other words, Drum Jr.'s mental orbit was quite a conventional, conservative one. And, as must have become quite clear by now, he never had much imagination. To be open to other people's points of view wasn't part of his *Weltanschauung*. But like his father before him, he felt always compelled to inflict his very fixed opinions of the world onto others. Another distinctive pattern that became evident was that, once he had made up his mind, it was almost impossible for him to change it. To be wrong, was not something that ever crossed his mind. To admit that it could be the case would make him feel totally lessened and humiliated. In addition, part of the autocratic "package" that he represented was a pattern of anti-intellectualism, expressed in the stark, oversimplified language that he would always resort to—the language he also used to denigrate others. In addition, Drum Jr. would always express himself in hyperbole: everything was always great, terrific, fantastic, and perfect. No wonder that Drum Jr. related very well to less educated people.

Paranoid Thinking

Furthermore, and not to forget, there was also Drum Jr.'s rather paranoid outlook on the world. Given his peculiar educational trajectory, the reader shouldn't be surprised to hear that he would see conspiracies everywhere. And if there wasn't anything to be suspicious about, he made sure to make it happen. It was a behavior pattern that he had very much perfected while being at the military academy. Of course, given his endless provocations, there was some truth to the idea that there were always people out to get at him. After all, we know that in Drum Jr.'s self-created world, life was a zero-sum game with winners and losers. And heaven forbid he should ever become a loser.

In addition, given his rather paranoid outlook on life, Drum Jr. was in the habit of slotting people into rigid categories, resulting in a split world with people who were for him or against him. It would always be like "us" versus "them." For Drum Jr., there was never a middle ground. And this stark way of dividing the world was also expressed in his strange fears of contagion, comparing out-groups to parasites, poisons, and other impurities. In this regard, it was no accident that throughout his life, Drum Jr. had a phobia of germs and would also be repulsed by bodily fluids, especially those of women.

Notwithstanding his very considerable flaws, on first impression, Drum Jr. could come across as quite charming and even charismatic. Unfortunately, this favorable impression didn't last very long. Very soon, given the damaged personality that he was, he would wear out his welcome. Most people would become annoyed, if not infuriated, given his need to be the center of attention. Whatever topic he breached, it would always become self-referential. It would always end up being about him. If no attention were paid, he would quickly get bored. Subsequently, he would resort to outrageous behavior for the seemingly simple purpose of being noticed. And if everything else failed, he would get other people's attention through threats and quarrels—his paranoid outlook coming to the rescue. Furthermore, what also could become extremely irritating, as a "*besserwisser*" (a person who would always know better), Drum Jr. would try to "colonize" other people's minds—trying to force people to agree with him. Like his father, he would harass them with his idiosyncratic view of the world, a pattern of behavior that would end up grating on everyone.

A Master of Factoids

Due to Drum Jr.'s distorted inner world, behaving in a straightforward manner would never be part of his makeup. Whenever a fact didn't suit him, he would change it in such a way that it would fit his particular way of looking at things. Actually, Drum Jr. had become a shameless master of "factoids," of creating alternative realities. Everything always needed to be his way. And as must have become clear by now to the reader, given his psychological makeup, he was truly a natural when it came to lying. Lying was his way of life. Anything would go. In that respect, principles were for others, not for him. Shocking, melodramatic, confounding lies would always be a regular weapon in his arsenal. In dealing with Drum Jr., people never knew what the truth was and what was a lie. And when he didn't get his way—when people refused to listen to his lies—he might have a tantrum, threatening to ruin the other party if he didn't get what he wanted. His outbursts of rage were legendary.

Drum Jr.'s cavalier attitude toward the truth was also a pattern in all his business dealings. As a businessman, trust would be mostly lacking. Whenever an opportunity arose, he would try to take advantage of other people. He would always try to pull a fast one. No wonder, as time went by, that as a businessman, Drum Jr. had gotten a reputation of being completely unreliable and unprincipled, always prepared to break whatever deal had been agreed upon.

Later, some psychologists would suggest that many of his grandiose, at times delusional, ideas and behavior should be looked at as a defense against deep-seated negative feelings about himself. He tended to "project" his anxieties onto others. He would accuse others of what he feared in himself. These psychologists even tried to point out that these dramatic antics should also be seen as manic maneuvers to fill up his inner emptiness. And without saying it out loud, many of the people who dealt with him thought that much of his behavior was extremely infantile. He was still very much the little kid, submitting to his father's wishes.

All in all, whatever Drum Jr. was trying to be, he was an unpleasant person to be with. With the passing of time, he had turned into a cunning, callous, cynical, and Machiavellian young man. At every occasion, he would try to inflate his wealth and business success, not forgetting to name all the beautiful women who were sexually attracted to him.

Anger Management

Another quality that typified Drum Jr.—the other emotional core around which his personality would constellate—was anger. It was anger that would permeate all his rhetoric. Anger would always be present, like a live volcano smoldering underneath. Where all this anger came from, however, was another question. Was its root cause related to the frustration of being the extension of someone else? Would he have liked to have had real choices in life—to do what he would have liked to do, whatever that would be? Did he resent being an extension of his father?

Clearly, at an earlier stage of his life, Drum Jr. had been unable to express this resentment, given the important role his father played. Presently, however, could this anger be a replay of when he was his younger self, when he had no choice but to contain his emotions, when he was unable to be angry at his father? Now, as an adult, was it possible that he was "transferring" this lingering anger toward others every time he was reminded of a similar situation—albeit without it being a conscious process? Some psychologists tried to point out that these mental acrobatics might be the explanation for his regular explosions of anger, his disagreeableness, his erratic behavior, and his irrational outbursts.

Whatever the origins, it was for all to see how Drum Jr.'s anger also compelled him to act out in strange ways. Furthermore, it was noticeable how this simmering anger was affecting other parts of his behavior. For example, whatever little sense of humor he possessed, it would always be expressed in a highly aggressive manner. It would always be used with the purpose of denigrating other people—it always had a very off-putting quality. Again, it added to the remarkably disagreeable personality "package" that Drum Jr. represented: a person who was callous, rude, arrogant, and lacking in empathy. To understand other people's feelings would always be beyond him. Being empathic was not part of his mental makeup.

Of course, while in the past, people had to face Drum Jr.'s raw anger—when he used his fists—when he felt crossed, in adulthood, he would use his attorneys to get his way. And these legal fights could be endless given his expertise in creating conflicts. It was like he had discovered a new contact sport. In his business dealings, Drum Jr. would constantly file lawsuit after lawsuit, defying those who would hold him to contracts. And as he would say many times publicly, when someone would attack him, he would always attack back, but he'll do it a hundred times more.

Driving Other People Crazy

With his formative years behind him, it now remained Drum Jr.'s challenge to pursue his father's quest to put the Drum name into the history books. The initial augurs to fulfill this quest weren't very positive as his adult life (as we have seen) had been characterized by broken marriages, busted businesses, and the ridicule of the people who got to know him. But whatever unethical messes he created, there always seemed to be a Teflon quality to him. In spite of his many misadventures, nothing ever seemed to stick. Whatever his misadventures, Drum Jr. would continue his merry, destructive ways.

In spite of his father's unusual educational program, we should recognize, however, that Drum Jr. wasn't completely without qualities. As a negotiator, he did have certain talents. When needed, he could be extremely tenacious. Especially, in making deals, his unusual toughness would shine through. He would always hang in there; he would rarely quit fighting. In that respect, in getting his adversaries off balance, Drum Jr. was very much his father's son. He knew how to wear the opposition down. He also knew how to drive them crazy by making one outlandish demand after another. Making concessions had never been part of his makeup. Given his zero-sum game attitude to life, Drum Jr. always believed that "The Art of the Deal" implied denigrating the competition. Whenever he had the opportunity, he would bargain hard on even the most trivial items of disagreement. And being the talented liar that he was, even if he didn't get what he wanted, he would pretend that he still had gotten his way. Unfortunately, however, the expression "penny wise and pound foolish" never came to his mind. Frequently, he might have appeared to be the winner, but by taking a very narrow perspective, he ended up being the real loser. Most of the people he dealt with never ever wanted to deal with him again. But it never dawned on Drum Jr. that his style of negotiating was not the way to build a good reputation.

In spite of all his spectacular failures, throughout his business career, Drum Jr. would present himself as a creative entrepreneur, as a talented risk-taker. In reality, as mentioned before, it was others (especially his father) who were taking the risks. Later on, whenever possible, he would try to put the risk off on everyone else, on all the lenders and banks, all the way down to the lowest tradesmen and subcontractors whom he would refuse to pay when it suited him, always readily finding excuses. Again, in spite of all these peccadilloes, he was quite talented in spinning all these failures into successes. It was imperative to him that whenever anything would go wrong, he couldn't be blamed. It always had to be the others. Clearly, the way Drum Jr. mentally rationalized his behavior indicated that he needed to be the winner at all costs. But in talking about his imaginary success stories, it eluded him that there is not much risk if you come into the world wealthy, insulated, and with substantial financial clout from the time you're in diapers.

What Persona?

Given Drum Jr.'s clownish, often amoral behavior, some people wondered who was really behind the mask. What was the real Drum like? Was there more to him than just appearances? What did he really stand for? Could he tell a meaningful story of what his life was all about? Were there any principles that were guiding him, except immediate self-interests? Was there more to him than was seen at first sight? Unfortunately, when pressed on the matter, what became evident was that he only cared about superficiality and glitter. Also, it would always end up Drum playing Drum, always fighting to win, but never knowing exactly why—with the only motivation being his desperate need to get people's attention.

Sadly enough, Drum Jr. had become an actor in a play, being always on stage. But he was acting in a play that was designed by his father. And although it had been many years since Old Drum had passed away, it was like his father was always hovering above, reminding him that he needed to make the Drum name famous for eternity—telling him that he had been chosen as the emissary to make it happen. And Drum Jr. obliged, playing this role in an outgoing, exuberant, and socially dominant manner. Most likely, his father's script in his inner theater explained his restlessness, his domineering style, and his compulsive need to be forever in the limelight. It also explained his relentless showmanship. It threw light on his wish to be a larger-than-life celebrity. In fact, some of this celebrity status he did acquire by participating in a reality TV show where he played the role of a successful entrepreneur deciding the fate of aspiring ones.

Running for King

As it happened, the king of Drum Jr.'s country died without any descendants. As was the law in the kingdom, all of its citizens, if they so desired, could throw their hat in the ring to become the new king. Clearly, for Drum Jr. the moment he had been waiting for all his life had at last arrived. The search for a new king would be his opportunity to achieve what his father had always wanted. If he were to become the king, the greatness of the Drums would be there for all to see. As king, the Drum name would go into the history books. Also, as Drum Jr. told himself, as king he would finally get the respect and admiration that he had always been craving for. As king, people would know how special he really was.

What also came to mind was that, as king, he could organize a coronation with himself as the central player. An event like that would truly lift his spirits. Wouldn't it be great to have so many people cheering him on, telling him how great he was? Besides, he thought, if his father would still be alive, wouldn't he be impressed? With these images passing his mind, Drum Jr. also thought how proud his mother would have been to look at all the pageantry that would be connected to his coronation. Actually, the more he thought about it, being king was so much more glorious than just trying to be a celebrity TV star. In addition, what also tickled his fancy, as king he could create one spectacle after the other. What a great way to have people pay attention to him.

Most people thought, however, that Drum Jr., given his terrible track record, was foolish to present himself as candidate for king. Even though he had turned into some kind of minor celebrity due to his endless showmanship on this TV reality show, most people believed that there was too much lacking given his outlandish, fake, clownish behavior. They couldn't imagine him as a serious candidate. To start with, they thought, he didn't have the brains. Also, they noted, he didn't have the capacity for systemic thinking, a quality very much needed to run such a complex entity like a kingdom. Some also wondered whether he had a vision for the country, a sense of what direction it should take. Others even questioned whether he had the capacity for hard work. Hadn't he always been famous for winging it? For too many people in the kingdom, to have him become a king looked too much like a wild goose chase given his disagreeableness and outbursts of irrationality.

Of course, there were others who had an even darker view of young Drum. Given his often-unethical, amoral behavior, they were very worried that a person without qualities—an individual without principles—would become king. They remembered that even his sister had made devastating comments about him. Worried as many people were, they reminded everyone that his path had always been strewn with betrayed business associates, duped clients, ditched friends, broken marriages, and estranged family members. Therefore, when Drum Jr. announced his candidacy, some of these people even joined a "never-Drum" movement—calling attention to all these concerns. They also made it quite clear that, if he were chosen, he would be a danger to the country. Naturally, Drum Jr., as always overestimating his abilities, didn't see it that way. He seemed to be quite confident that he had a very good chance to win.

After all, he was the Teflon man. He could perpetuate scandal after scandal, but whatever he did, it would never stick.

The first thing Drum Jr. did, in trying to change all this negative talk about him, was to create a fictional double, a person who was talking secretly to the press, telling journalists how great he really was. Pretending to be someone else, he would tell them all the things he thought the general public would like to hear about him. Later, when this ruse was discovered, psychologists looked at this strange activity as a personal attempt at reparation—another symptom of not really feeling appreciated.

While playing the role of this imaginary double, Drum Jr. would tell them that he was the ideal person to make the country great again. Actually, if this double was to be believed, the country had apparently gone to pot under the previous regime. The secretive voice would add that the deceased king had been totally incompetent. And he would continue telling whoever was willing to listen how worrisome it was that the late king had not paid any attention to the many enemies circling the country. Also, he would whisper softly that there was a fifth column inside the country—groups of people eager to undermine what the country stood for. In addition, he would emphasize that the other candidates for king were totally corrupt. Interestingly enough, as a caveat in the context of using a fictional double as spokesperson, later when he became king, Drum Jr. would name his son by his third marriage after this imaginary double, perhaps a hesitant attempt to make fiction a reality.

Cleaning the Swamp

In public forums, Drum Jr. knew exactly how to cater to the people's wish to believe. He turned out to be a master in persuading the gullible. Quite knowledgeable about what populist leaders do, he was an expert in knowing how to milk popular aggrievements. He knew how to pick up lingering feelings of dissatisfaction with the country's present state of affairs. Subsequently, given his talents at demagoguery, he would present himself as the champion in addressing perceived wrongs. He was the one going to defend the people that felt victimized; that felt left behind. And as a good populist, while advocating his candidacy, he would promise the people in the country everything that they wished to hear, notwithstanding the outlandishness of most of these promises. Over and over, he would repeat the message that he was the only person to make the country great again.

According to Drum Jr., the country had been in steep decline far too long. To add to these words of gloom and doom, he would claim that dark clouds were appearing on the horizon, that enemies were encircling the country, and that their way of life was under threat. He would point out that the people in other countries were taking advantage of them; they were taking their jobs away. And while painting this rather dystopian future, he would assure all those willing to listen that the only thing that stood between them and the deluge would be him. He was the only person who could keep them safe. Only he would be able to protect them from the still more horrible things that might await them if they chose someone else, making very clear that the country would be very different if he would be elected king. As he would say repeatedly, to dramatically change the country nobody was more qualified. And his comments resonated with many—in particular uneducated, white males—as they felt that they were losing out in the lottery of life. It was as if their imagination was still dominated by times long gone when heroic, macho cowboys were fighting the bad guys. The words of Drum Jr., however, gave them hope for a better future.

Drum Jr. also vowed that if they made him king, his first step would be to build a wall to keep out all the bad people—the people who were threatening their way of life. According to him, there were too many bad "hombres"— these dangerous immigrants out there—who were out to destroy the country. Conveniently, Drum Jr. seemed to have forgotten that his paternal grandfather was an immigrant and so was his mother. Again, going into xenophobic overdrive, he pointed out repeatedly that nobody else was more qualified to deal with all these bad people. And while talking about all these made-up threats, he would repeat the message that the other candidates for king were weak, corrupt, and totally unreliable. He would stress that the present government was made up of extremely corrupt incompetents. As king, however, he would eradicate all corruption. He would clean up the swamp.

More than any other candidate, populist as he was, Drum Jr. knew how to stir up the emotions of his audience. He knew how to create real drama. And given all his theatrics, he even managed to build a cult of Drum followers who would end up believing and parroting every word he said. They bought into his world of alternative realities. Incredibly, whatever outlandish statements he would make, they remained among the believers. It seemed as though they lived to hear his words. They liked his melodramatics. They enjoyed his "fan facts." And for melodramatics, they couldn't have found a better person. Drum Jr. knew how to whip up his believers to act out aggressively toward all those standing in his way. He knew how to create drama, both internally and externally—being a real master of divisiveness. He knew how to divide people into camps that were for him and against him. Without being consciously aware of it, he turned out to be a master in crowd dynamics, seemingly knowing all the tricks to get people to identify with him—and follow him.

Furthermore, to add to his theatrics, Drum Jr. also told his followers that his opponents should be imprisoned, that they really should be locked up. Given what they had been doing—if he was to be believed—they were really "enemies of the people," a line he seemed to have borrowed from demagogues before him. Furthermore, while running for king, he was also developing a whole shopping list of enemies. Of course, among his most preferred ones were journalists who wrote unfavorable reports about him. Repeatedly, he would accuse them of being a totally corrupted bunch, paid to write bad things about him.

Some people commented, however, that it was like Drum Jr. (without even realizing it) was talking about himself. As had long been his pattern, he was projecting onto the outside that which was happening on the inside. Given his track record, wasn't he really the corrupted, unreliable one? Wasn't he always pulling a fast one on everyone he ever dealt with? But in spite of the irony of it all, many people found his doomsday messages extremely attractive. They were attracted to him since he was echoing many of the darker things they thought about in private, things they imaged were happening in the country.

The King of Drumlandia

To many people's surprise, his dark message about the dangers threatening the kingdom hit home. Gullible as many people can be, there were those who began to believe his promise that he was really the only one who could save the kingdom from disaster, that he was the ideal person to make the country great again. Clearly, his divisive tactics, perfected when growing up, were working. As a grandmaster of misinformation, he knew how to incite the population to buy into his message. He had always known how to create alternative realities. In addition, as a way of getting attention, Drum Jr. captured people's attention given the many violent incidents at his election rallies aimed at people who objected to his demagoguery. And the ruthless way he handled these situations persuaded his devotees that he had the toughness required to become king. Very surprisingly, even though it was with a very slim margin, Drum Jr. won the contest. Now, many people in the kingdom were becoming very nervous wondering what was going to happen next.

Once Drum became king, he was over the moon having finally reached the stage on which he had always wanted to perform. Pleased with himself, he knew that, given his present position, everybody had no choice but to pay attention. Finally, the time had come when he could make his mark. The moment had come when he could show everyone how great a Drum really was.

Given King Drum's opening moves, it didn't take long to convince people that there had never been a person as consistently and overtly disagreeable on the public stage as him. And in playing the role of an SOB, in that respect King Drum turned out to be very much his father's son. Soon after his coronation, a remarkable set of cruel policies aimed at the weak and vulnerable was announced as a first sign of things to come. Any official who objected to the measures that he was putting into place was immediately dismissed. And to make clear to his subjects what he stood for, there was also a constant stream of short edicts sent to the media, presenting his latest views on whatever caught his fancy. Mostly, what he came up with were hateful messages, containing negative comments about anybody standing in his way. Given his busyness during the night in preparing these messages, some people began to wonder whether their new king was suffering from insomnia. Did he have troublesome dreams that needed to find an outlet through his many edicts?

Living in an Echo Chamber

Having reached the most important position in the kingdom, King Drum had finally attained a stage in his life where he could show everyone that he was the best thing that could have happened to them. The moment had come for all to accept how brilliant, powerful, and magnificent he really was.

Given King Drum's preoccupation with himself, it didn't take very long before many of his courtiers realized that the prescription to get their king into a good mood was to tell him that he was the greatest. To survive, they better play the role of sycophants. They came to accept that he liked to start every meeting of his senior officials expecting an almost worshipful praise by them. He wanted all of them to express what a great honor it was to be working for him. And as his inner circle was learning quickly, it was a great way to get him on their side. In contrast, a lack of affirmation of his greatness could have serious consequences. Thus, not having much of a choice, they went along with this strange process, hoping that if King Drum was in a good mood, something could get done. Privately, however, many of them thought he was still very much behaving like a child. Also, they noted, very much like a small child, their new king would have regular tantrums if he didn't get this "fix." If he didn't get his regular dose of adulation, King Drum would quickly become morose and irritable.

As time passed, for many of his subjects, King Drum's neediness became grinding. They realized that he had to constantly self-aggrandize to defend himself against feelings of emptiness and imagined narcissistic injuries. Taking excessive credit for any success while blaming others for his failures only seemed to temporarily lift his spirits. Whatever heroic deeds his courtiers attributed to him, they would never be good enough. In spite of the many positive comments, what was said was never sufficient for positive feelings to last very long. Instead, these messages needed to be repeated over and over again. It made his courtiers realize that being with King Drum was like walking on eggshells. At any moment, there could be a breaking point. Outbursts of rage were the order of the day. There was always something that was causing his ire. And they knew that his rage could have terrible consequences. No wonder that his vindictiveness became legendary. People were fired left and right. King Drum expected total loyalty. Any sign of it not being the case would end up in dramatic action.

Given King Drum's behavior, many started to wonder whether the expression "pride goeth before the fall" also applied to him. Given all his antics, what was going to happen to the kingdom? Could he be trusted with the precious heirloom that was the country? Was he truly making the country great or was he really just doing the opposite? What was the future going to look like? To many, it looked like dark clouds were appearing on the horizon.

Paranoia Being the Disease of Kings

As the years passed, King Drum became known far and wide for the cunning, callous, cynical, and Machiavellian style in which he was running the country. Everything he did, just as he had been taught by his father, was looked at through the prism of money. The costs and benefits of making decisions were seen in purely financial terms—morality and ethics be damned.

Sitting on his throne, surrounded by his sycophants, with the unfinished business of his past staring out from the framed photos of his parents, King Drum was dragging the country through his personal psychodrama, having him lash out pitiless when he felt misunderstood. And as he had become the main actor in this psychodrama, many of his actions would acquire a surrealistic quality. More than ever before, King Drum's subjects were asking themselves which of his statements were true and which were false. Whatever announcements he made, his comments would always be extremely confusing. And, unfortunately, his tendency to annihilate the distinction between what was true and what was false would only increase as time went by. As lying had always come naturally to him, in his role as king, he became a greater disseminator of misinformation. And it became more dangerous, given the role model he presented in being the king. Others would imitate his behavior.

Of course, what shone through the many lies would always be his insatiable ego, his inability to take real responsibility, his unreliability, his distrust of everyone, and his callous disregard for the future. The only rationale his subjects could discern behind all this irrational behavior was his insatiable need to be admired, and to be seen as the greatest. Everything he did would always have a self-referential quality. Like his father before him, any discussion with him turned out to be a strange, rather egotistical dialogue.

Due to King Drum's behavior, trust had become a rare commodity in the kingdom. Increasingly, people came to distrust whatever their king had to say. On a personal level, the only people he seemed to trust, granted only to a degree, were his children. But even they, in dealing with the king, would be walking on eggshells, always knowing that it was in their best interest to completely agree with him. They knew, like his minions had discovered the hard way, that as long as they said what he liked to hear (very similar to the way King Drum had behaved with his father) they might be able to get what they wanted. Over time, however, his children and in-laws had learned to play this game quite well. It explained why his reliance on his family would always be on full display, but also leading to many financial conflicts of interest. Thus, ironically, as a supposedly anti-corruption candidate, many of his subjects were becoming increasingly perturbed at how his adult children and their spouses were having an unprecedented influence over his decisions to the detriment of his appointed advisers. Many suspected that they were taking financial advantage of their position.

What many began to recognize was King Drum's deep-seated sense of victimhood, a characteristic that once helped him relate to his many followers who felt victimized about what life had been offering them. But given King Drum's own delicate mental equilibrium, it didn't take much to have him also feel misunderstood. While talking to his sycophants, he would constantly complain about the fact that his subjects just didn't understand all the good things he was doing for the country. According to him, given all the great things he had done, most of them were just an ungrateful bunch. They never gave him sufficient credit. They never praised him the way they should.

To add to this sense of victimhood—given his paranoid disposition—King Drum also imagined that people were after him, that there were many people out to get him—not a very surprising observation. Throughout his life, he had very much taken to heart the expression "only the paranoid survive!" And

3 The Little Drum Boy or the Rise and Fall of a Flawed Leader 65

even when there was no reason to be paranoid, he always had been very talented in creating enemies where there were none. Expectedly, however, given his paranoid outlook, he always believed that even his most trusted advisers were conspiring against him. It explained, given this particular state of mind, why he would regularly get rid of them. It was for this reason that there was a constant turnover among the members of his inner circle. And given his perverse selection criteria, many of them ended up in prison, being charged with corruptive practices.

Of course, given his position as king, there was a degree of reality in his notion of being suspicious. After all, as said before, paranoia is the disease of kings. But in the case of King Drum, his suspicion really was over the top. And given his previously mentioned tendency to split the world into "us" versus "them" categories, it wasn't difficult for him to find imagined enemies everywhere. As it always had come naturally to him to blame others for any mishap, it was easy to find people who he perceived as being against him. Thus, always projecting on others what he feared in himself, he was accusing others of many of the things he was actually responsible for. Soon, people in the know came to realize that taking personal responsibility for failed actions would never be part of his agenda. King Drum would never imagine that he might be the originator of his own misery.

In characterizing the people King Drum perceived as being against him, he consistently relied on such extreme terms as bad, dirty, and destructive. Increasingly, instead of trying to unite the country, he became a master of divisiveness. Under his leadership the country became evermore divided. Hatefulness would always be his preferred way of rallying his base. If King Drum was to be believed, many enemies were encircling the country. And to make his subjects understand the forces he imagined himself up against, he would use in his speeches the simplistic language of stark opposites. Here, his talent in giving people denigrating nicknames was coming to good use. Given the way he would rant and rave, many people came to understand that it had to be a very dark world King Drum lived in. It always turned out to be a world of black and white—of good against evil. But what was considered "evil" was another question!

Furthermore, given his notion of always feeling misunderstood, there were various occasions when King Drum would seem totally unhinged. Too often, his courtiers experienced how the slightest mishap could lead to extremely angry outbursts. In such instances, full of rage, he would be slashing out. It made many of them realize how much anger was always smoldering within him. But given the enormous power of the office, his behavior was perceived as being very scary. Also, what scared them, when these angry outbursts occurred, was that they would not only lead to strange decisions, but also to violent acts.

As time went by, King Drum's mood swings had become legendary. People close to him realized that his decisions were becoming increasingly erratic, up to the point of complete irrationality. Unhinged as he could be, there were many occasions when he seemed to be unable to follow the thread of a conversation, when he ended up jumping from topic to topic. Some even wondered whether it was the consequence of a lifetime of unprocessed, unacknowledged anxiety, exacerbated by the power and responsibility of the office. Whatever the reason was, when King Drum entered such a state, there was nobody who could calm him down. While having a tantrum, no adult in the room could do anything about it. There seemed to be nobody with the courage to set boundaries. Everyone who had tried to do so had already been fired.

Hubris Comes Before the Fall

As time passed by, not only King Drum's inner circle but also his subjects realized that he wasn't really interested in bettering their lives. A much better description would be that he was more interested in bettering his own life. They recognized that his main driver had always been his insatiable need for recognition. Drum had always been about Drum. Rarely, while in pursuit of personal glory, would his concerns dovetail with pressing societal issues. Like it had always been for him in the past, all his decisions were guided by his idiosyncratic, amoral, extremely self-centered view of the world. Strategic thinking had never been his forte. King Drum was never able to operate according to specific agendas or organizing principles. Given his autocratic leadership style, listening to the advice of others on how to make the country truly a great place was not on his "to do" list.

If there would be one organizing principle, however, it was the maintenance of his powerbase. At all costs, King Drum wanted to prevent the slightest challenge to his rule. For that purpose, he had created a small mafia-like inner core mainly made up of old cronies and selected family members. In addition, he also knew how to use financial incentives to encourage his security forces, both military and police, to protect the regime while at the same time having them monitor each other. And while he was putting all these measures into place, he was pretending that he had his constituency's best interests at heart. For many people, however, this façade of being really a servant leader was quickly wearing down. Although King Drum may have had some popular appeal at the beginning of his reign, with the passing of the years, his popularity had taken a deep dive, the exception being the members of the Drum cult. Thus, as far as his base was concerned, by creating much drama, while propagating divisiveness, he was able to continue his appeal. They continued to believe anything he said.

At this point in King Drum's rule, it was for most people to see that the dramatic antics that had propelled him to rise to the position of king weren't helpful in running the country. Perhaps the overestimation of his abilities may have been attractive when lobbying for the position of king, but presently, facing the reality of what it meant to run a kingdom, King Drum was felt greatly wanting. And as day-to-day leadership never had any interest for him, an increasing number of people started to question his leadership capabilities. The disparity between the competencies needed to run the country and his complete incompetence were becoming increasingly glaring, highlighting King Drum's troubled personality more than ever before. It was for all to see that King Drum had no idea of and very little interest in what it meant to run the country.

Also, another very worrisome development was the lack of a competent inner circle. The more competent courtiers had discovered quite quickly that King Drum didn't listen to their advice. Whatever advice they were trying to give him, when it didn't fit his interest of the day, it was ignored. Consequently, most of them, completely disillusioned with his behavior, were fired or had left. Those who stayed came to understand that King Drum wanted only to hear what he liked to hear. They realized it was in their best interest not to bring him any bad news. Never should they bring him any information that would disrupt the image of popularity and success that he had constructed for himself. Thus, as they discovered, it was imperative that they censored all the information brought to him. As they had experienced far too often, they knew that he would react with fury if he heard that he wasn't as popular as he used to be. To King Drum, his popularity ratings were always of the utmost importance.

Eventually, fearful of his dramatic behavior, King Drum's courtiers—being talented "enablers"—constructed some kind of bubble around him as a way of insulating him from bad news, negative feedback, and pretty much any form of criticism. The tragic outcome of protecting him from disturbing news was, however, that he was increasingly unable to respond to the changing national mood, incapable of adjusting to a public that was asking for more leadership and less theater. This led to a situation whereby he could no longer see what was happening right in front of him. King Drum was getting badly out of step with the national psyche.

Eventually, many members of King Drum's close entourage also came to realize that the constant threat of his self-righteous, out-of-control rage was becoming increasingly dangerous, given the public stage he was operating on. Any inkling of possible humiliation had him lash out for revenge, which was more often than not an extremely exaggerated response to imaginary insults. And with the way things were going, many of them feared that his actions could easily escalate—to completely run out of control. They recognized that King Drum's autocratic leadership style that fed on divisiveness and external threats could have catastrophic outcomes. The dystopian world he had created for himself could turn into a self-fulfilling prophecy. After all, painting doomsday scenarios had always been his unique way of justifying his rule in the country. Making Jeremiah-like statements had given him the opportunity to present himself as the defender of the kingdom. But given his position—and given his mercurial temperament—many feared that when his popularity as king would become questionable, he could become truly dangerous. They were concerned that, as a way of igniting new enthusiasm for his activities, he would not only be tempted to incite more internal strife, but also be prepared to start external strife in the form of a war. Many people were becoming increasingly worried about what was to come.

Gotterdämmerung

As time went on, a decreasing number of his subjects were prepared to buy into King Drum's abusive behavior. Gradually, he was becoming more and more isolated. Finding competent people who were willing to work for him was becoming very difficult. Too many of them had come and gone. Working at the court had turned into a never-ending rotating door. While early in his reign, some of these people may have had a degree of admiration for him— even trying to rationalize some of his crazy ideas—that notion had long past. His behavior had become too outrageous. They realized how his irrational antics were hurting the country. King Drum had become a toxic entity. Every time he would open his mouth, his words became even more divisive.

While in King Drum's earlier days some people were attracted to him by being close to the source of power (with all its perks and other benefits), that attraction had also long gone. Most of them were all too aware of the high reputational price they had to pay in being associated with him. They recognized that King Drum's poor judgment, born of overconfidence combined with an unwillingness to consider information that did not suit his worldview, was leaving too many damaged systems and relationships in its wake. Many realized that the noble idea of modifying his excessive behavior had been nothing but an illusion. When King Drum was on to something, he was unstoppable.

In light of the kingdom's decline, King Drum's demands for unquestionable loyalty and devotion had become unsustainable. Moreover, an increasing number of his subjects began to see him as a threat to the kingdom. All along, during his short rule, he had disappointed far too many people. While in the past his unflappable self-confidence had him labeled as charismatic, due to his complete self-centeredness that idea was dropped a long time ago. His many deceptions and intimidations were becoming just too disturbing. His inflated sense of self, his need for constant tribute from others, his hypersensitivity to any form of criticism, his shallow emotional attachments, his lack of empathy, his exploitative actions, his coldness and ruthlessness, his rigidity in outlook, and his paranoid view of the world were clearly evident. What was also there for all to see was that his ego had become so inflated that in his pursuit of self-interest, he had stopped even pretending that he was doing anything in the interest of the nation. King Drum never seemed to have realized that it is important to tame your ego before your ego tames you.

Still, some of his subjects continued to think that it would be best to just let it be. Even though the behavior of King Drum was more than unconventional, at least the kingdom was still prospering. Financially, some continued to believe that some of the things he was doing were of benefit to them. Opportunistically they thought why not stay with him? Of course, what some economists were all too ready to point out that he was having a lucky run without having really done anything substantial to make the economy work. Others, although bothered by the amorality of many of his actions, continued to try not to see what was happening. They rationalized their complicity. And they thought why not enjoy the good life.

But as strife became an increasingly common pattern in the country, many of King Drum's subjects felt that bread alone was no longer good enough. His unethical, often ruthless ways of doing things began to grind on many of them. Although some still saw some short-term opportunistic financial benefits in having him as king, many of his subjects had become greatly disillusioned. In particular, they were missing a sense of dignity. And what added oil to the fire was the callous behavior of the people who were still hanging on to him. Some of the "leftovers" of King Drum's inner circle seemed to be inspired by his antics. They were "identifying with the aggressor"; they were copying his behavior. The king's bullying and threatening way of going about things had become very contagious.

Furthermore, as expected, King Drum's belligerent language, imitated by his hangers-on, had become quite irritating to the rival nations at whom they were taking aim. Given the provocative language they were using, the countries surrounding the kingdom were affected. Thus, not only did his actions create internal strife, but his divisiveness also contributed to external unrest. Again, he was doing everything but making the country great again. Instead, the country was becoming the laughingstock of other nations. King Drum had become an incredible embarrassment. Many people in the kingdom started to realize that King Drum was greatly damaging the country's reputation.

People's concerns reached an all-time high when a pandemic struck the country. Again, King Drum's reaction to the situation was as expected. He resorted to massive denial, pretending that there was no cause for worry. He would announce that, whatever sort of thing this pandemic was, it would soon just fade away. It was just like the flu. In the meantime, hundreds of thousands of people were dying. King Drum didn't seem to realize that giving nasty nicknames to whoever stood in his way—the way he had always been demonizing his opponents—wouldn't work when faced with a pandemic. This time, he was dealing with a very different opponent.

Given his actions or better lack of action, his subjects realized that the emperor had really no clothes. Although members of the Drum cult were still standing behind him, others were now truly worried that the cult of personality that King Drum had created could be the beginning of a possible tyranny. They were concerned that, if he felt threatened, he might well descend further into abuse and authoritarianism as a way to reassert his power.

Furthermore, as these were very trying times, people had become totally fed up with the spirit of divisiveness and chaos that King Drum had created, that nothing was planned or under control. It may have once served a purpose to have his followers unite behind his ideas, but now this attraction was wearing out fast with so many people dying. Many came to realize how hollow his worldview really was. They also recognized how expendable they were when King Drum was in need of scapegoats. And even though, at one time, they may have enjoyed the way he had been breaking the norms on how a king should behave, his outrageous behavior wasn't working any longer. An increasing number of people believed that he was totally unfit to rule as a king. Increasingly, they came to see him as unhinged and dangerous. Some even said that he had become "psycho" or "deranged," whatever they meant by it.

Even though there were still a great number of "enablers," many of King Drum's other subjects saw the light. Only now did it start to dawn on them that King Drum was a person of all talk and no real action. They now saw him for what he really was: erratic, irrational, foolish, uninformed, and stunningly incompetent. And to add to this sad package, they realized that he was also very lazy. He spent too much of his time on the golf course, not bothering to deal with the affairs of state.

No longer blinded by all the noise he had been making, people were hard-pressed to identify any significant decision that wasn't driven by the simple motivation to stroke his ego. People who were in the know noted that King Drum's thinking was really like an archipelago of dots, leaving it to others to try to put these dots together to arrive at some kind of policy decisions. Many of them were now prepared to talk about his corruptive influence—how many of his actions had as their only purpose the aim to enrich himself and the members of his family. Finally, they came to realize that instead of having chosen a man of iron, they had chosen a man of pasteboard.

Given these changes in the mood of the population, the original bargain between King Drum and his subjects was collapsing rapidly. His increasingly coercive tactics to make up for the shortfall in public trust caused by its xenophobic policies, his baiting of opponents, and his encouragement of police violence were increasingly resented. Whipping up the fear factor was losing its effectiveness. Earlier it had always been easy for King Drum to demonize outsiders as vectors of disease, death, and economic disintegration. In the past, he had always received a pass for not dealing with facts and reason, but rather with the brute force that would make his word law, unencumbered by anything but his own will. But with so many people dying, these tactics had lost their effectiveness. In particular, his subjects found it unforgiveable that he was pooh-poohing the pandemic. Even his close allies wondered why he wasn't even able to fake a sense of compassion about the suffering of his people. Clearly, people were turning against the chaos, cruelty, deception, and incompetence induced by their king. People began to complain publicly. Rebellion was in the air.

Most kings will have a few embittered people. As king, it will always be impossible to please everyone. Unfortunately, King Drum had entered into a very different league. As things stood now, he faced not only an exodus of disgruntled courtiers, but also that of many alarmed officials at all kinds of institutions and all corners of his government. Many of them whispered how crazy he really was. Many of them were willing to state out loud that he was a danger to the kingdom. But as was to be expected, when some of these concerns reached the ears of King Drum, it made him even meaner and more erratic. Firing people left and right, the revolving door in his government began to turn faster and faster. The king was burning through people like a pyromaniac. And many of the people he dismissed left quite revengefully.

These people realized, however, that revenge was a dish always best served on the media. And while they were watching how their king was falling apart, their voices on the media became stronger and stronger. The weaker their king seemed to be, the chattier they became. They were telling all those willing to listen how petty, incompetent, and idiotic King Drum really was.

The lightning rod for mass unrest was the savage beating of a number of demonstrators by King Drum's secret police. The incident led to even greater demonstrations against his reign, disturbances that, once again, he tried to suppress violently. This time, however, he wasn't as successful. The greater part of the population had become emboldened. They were no longer letting it be but continued to protest against his rule. The way King Drum had been suppressing his people was no longer working. He could no longer plug the channels of criticism; he could no longer control the free flow of information.

As things developed in the kingdom, King Drum's public image was taking a deep dive. Now openly, the population of the country was questioning the king's competence to rule. Also, with so many people dying, even his original supporters were deserting him in droves. A few blinded believers excluded—the general population was no longer attracted to the kind of ideology that had led to his rise to power. They were fed up with all the hatred he had been sowing. Finally, they saw him for what he really was: a total fake. In his role as king, they now realized, he never had a real message to give to his people beyond expressing his personal grievances. As king, he had never done anything meaningful to make the country great. In fact, the opposite was true, as many came to realize.

To continue this tale of woe, the "coup-proofing" strategy of King Drum, of having created a small mafia-like inner core mainly made up of his old cronies and selected family members, was falling apart. The incentives he had used to buy the support of the security forces, both military and police, to protect the regime was also no longer working. In spite of the financial benefits they were receiving, at long last, even his original loyalists had become fed up.

Predictably, while all these changes were happening, King Drum—living in his own echo chamber—being the creator of a distorted reality field, didn't really understand what was happening around him. Instead of taking reality-based actions, he continued to live in a fantasy world, believing that he still enjoyed the support of his people. Actually, being coddled in his isolation, surrounded by the few remaining sycophants, immersed in his own sense of essentialness, King Drum was the last to know that things were falling apart. He kept on insisting that his people still loved him. And he even argued that the polls that showed him sinking underwater were nothing but fake news. At the same time, however, his nagging apprehension that he no longer would be sufficiently attractive or powerful, as well as his fear of failure, only increased his penchant for bullying, making his behavior even more violent. The scariest thing about King Drum was this unique combination of ignorance about the world, combined with a great ignorance about himself.

To end this tale of woe, King Drum's tragic errors of judgment had plunged the country into a nightmare. And as we have seen in so many fairy tales, ignorance can be lethal. To finish this tale, there was much violence that was instigated by him. Given the violence, many people died. Also, taking a financial perspective, many people faced ruin. Many of them descended into poverty. What added to this miserable scenario was the fact that their king had failed in his primary duty to keep his citizens safe. The pandemic raged on, adding to the worrisome death toll. Not surprisingly, people's trust in the government was broken. In addition, the country's relationships with its surrounding nations had reached its lowest point ever. Actually, looking at what was happening with their once mighty neighbor, these other countries even pitied King Drum's subjects. They wondered why on Earth the population had ever been so foolish as to choose him as their leader. King Drum had been doing everything not to make his country great again. Instead, what they could see was a shell-shocked nation with an extremely distraught population. They even considered what had once been an exemplary nation now was turning into some kind of "banana republic." Too many of the things that had once been beyond their wildest imagination had in fact happened.

Predictably, as has been the case in so many fairy tales, heroes—or more accurately, villains—who live by a despotic ego will fall by a despotic ego. In that respect, this is not the kind of fairy tale where people live happily ever after. The sad ending of this tragic tale is that King Drum wallowing in self-pity, still thinking in his uniquely delusional way whereby he was God's gift to the kingdom and never realizing how he had bungled up his chance to be a much-loved king, was thrown into the garbage bin of obscurity. And predictably, he didn't go quietly. After all, we all know that malignant narcissists always need to win. To these people, losing would always be perceived as a total catastrophe—the end of the world—which would make them do anything to prevent it from happening. Given his upbringing, losing for King Drum had always been unimaginable.

To prevent his fall from power, at every turn, King Drum tried to overturn the will of the people. Everything, he imagined, was permissible to maintain what he thought was his God-given right to rule, including a scorched earth strategy. As was expected, he tried to unleash even more violence in the country, a tactic, he hoped, would enable him to present himself as the savior. He even tried to enlist the help of the country's top military and political leaders to keep him in power. Unfortunately for him, most of them decided to take a pass. Most of them saw through his schemes, refusing to act on it. Finally, they thought, enough was enough. Still, there were violent protests of the members of the Drum cult. More people died. In the end, however, sanity prevailed. Most people realized the danger that he represented—how unhinged their king really was; how what was a constitutional monarchy could easily be turned into a very dark tyranny; how their king had failed his people.

Even when all was said and done, and he had no chance to continue his reign, King Drum never understood his own failings. He still refused to leave. He still didn't accept that he had to go. Finally, totally unhinged, kicking, and screaming, he was dragged from his throne. It was the antithesis of an exit with dignity. And although some members of the Drum cult continued to protest violently, his reign of terror had passed.

Interestingly enough, to create some kind of "happy" ending, instead of taking recourse to regicide, his subjects decided to send King Drum into exile. Being in a forgiving mood, they deported him to an island far, far away, hoping that he would never be heard of again. But notwithstanding him being in exile, rumors were still going around that their fallen king was dabbling in magic, perhaps as a way of trying to make a comeback or to put an evil spell on the kingdom. Obviously, however, as nothing happened, the magic didn't pay off. Some noted that their ex-king had always been a poor learner. Also, this time, there was no longer a father to bail him out.

Of course, given this sad ending, the question becomes whether King Drum ever fulfilled his father's quest. Did he make the name Drum famous? Actually, it is fair to say that he had made the name Drum infamous. Forever, he would be known as the worst king the kingdom ever had. In a somewhat convoluted way, we could label such an ending as even a happy one. After all, given his father's quest, isn't infamy also the antidote to obscurity?

For the reader, however, the challenge will be to tell this sad fairy tale to all aspiring leaders. Clearly, to be an effective leader will always be a challenge. And being in a leadership position isn't necessarily going to be a fairy tale with happy endings. As this fairy tale illustrates, fairy tale endings can come in all forms and manners. If truth be told, in real fairy tales, happy endings for leaders tend to be few and far between. Of course, it doesn't mean that leaders cannot have fairy tale moments.

Reflecting on King Drum's educational trajectory, apart from a leader's rise and fall, this fairy tale may have taught us also something about the making of a leader. Possibly, given his early history, it may also have evoked in the reader a dose of sympathy. It may have given us a modicum of understanding why King Drum turned into such a toxic entity. Some of the readers may even have felt some pity, as he had the misfortune to be subjected to a remarkable dysfunctional upbringing. Furthermore, what this story also has made quite clear is that living with parents like King Drum's isn't a fairy tale—and it will not make for fairy tale endings. It also makes us realize that nobody is born a monster. In fact, all of us are able to create monsters. And what's more, all of us may turn into monsters. Sometimes, however, we wish that they were just born as monsters; that nature overturns nurture. It would make it so much easier to hate these monsters.

As I said in the beginning of this story, from ancient times onward, people have invented fairy tales. Fairy tales have always been the medium, and the basis, for understanding problems, events, joy, pain, loss, and solace. The main purpose of most of these fairy tales has been, as I mentioned in this book's introduction, to present a moral that the reader should remember. Also, in fairy tales, people will be taking a journey; many of these stories are about transformation. They are also about self-improvement, making people aware of what morals are all about—something King Drum failed at miserably. We can also see how this fairy tale taught us something about society, relationships, emotions, values, vices, and for sure, good and evil. And what's convenient is that in fairy tales, good and evil tend to be presented in very stark colors. Gray areas are rarely to be found. Symbolically, this particular fairy tale also conveyed the experiences we go through as we navigate relationships toward developing our own identity—of what it means to be human, and how we face good and evil.

Furthermore, as can also be seen in the tale of King Drum, another purpose of fairy tales is to nurture our imagination. Fairy tales may encourage us to "dream big" and think of things that are magical and mystical. Some of these stories make us believe that anything is possible. They may help to recreate the creative imagination we once had as children. In that respect, fairy tales are the doorways to other realities. Imagination is what's really needed to be able to understand the strange tale of King Drum.

All in all, the fairy tale just told was really a horrendous nightmare for those who lived it, and a tale preferably forgotten by those who didn't. As I mentioned earlier, what this tale also told us is that monsters exist and can come to the fore—as well as how they can be beaten. Furthermore, this fairy tale reminds us never to become monsters ourselves.

Unfortunately, however, slaying the monster isn't what always happens in every fairy tale. And even if the monster were to be slain in the end, in the interim period—as we have seen in the tale of King Drum—many terrible things can happen. Too many fairy tales have a bloody lining. Perhaps, that's the reason why there are so few happy fairy tale endings in real life. But as the reader may have found out by now, what's important is not really the happy ending but the story. It is the warning contained in these fairy tales that counts. It is what makes fairy tales so important. It is why fairy tales help us to reflect deeply on the tragedies and difficulties of life.

Listening to this tale also makes us realize once more that fairy tales are not just for children. Fairy tales are really for all of us. Fairy tales contain the power not only to help us change, but also to transform the world around us. In this particular case, we were exposed to a fairy tale that warns us of the danger of toxic leaders—how to recognize one, never to become one, and never to create one. In spite of the tragedy found in this tale, even this fairy tale contains some hope. Yet, whether there is hope or not, it is my sincere wish that the tale I have told you will not become your tale. I hope you, the reader, have been in the wrong story. That you will act differently. And when you realize that you are really in the wrong story, you know enough to get out. That's the way life comes about.

This brings me to the next story. Again, it describes the antics of a populist leader—a person who unleashes hatred as a lever to gain power. The tale tells how hatred has caused many problems in this world of ours but hasn't solved a single one. Frankly speaking, this tale may help us understand that hatred only invites more hatred. In this context, I was reminded of a statement by the Buddha: "Hatred doesn't cease by hatred, but only by love; this is the eternal rule."

4

A Strange Tale of Hatred

Hate is a bottomless pit: I will pour and pour.
—Euripides

Hatred does not cease by hatred, but only by love; this is the eternal rule.
—Siddhārtha Gautama

Once upon a time, in another faraway land where people still had a sense of wonder, there lived a man called Bolsonaro who was known far and wide because of his vitriolic language. On every occasion, he would make the most outrageous, disturbing statements. Whatever the topic would be, his comments were always full of hatred. Listening to him, there seemed to be no end to all the people and things that troubled him. Bolsonaro's hateful behavior made many people wonder, however, why he acted in this manner. Where did all this hatred come from? Why was he so compelled to say all these hateful things?

If Bolsonaro would have been a person of no consequences, his comments could have been easily ignored. But that wasn't the case at all. He was the leader of the country. Given his position, many of the people listening to him thought him to be highly irresponsible for spouting all this hatred. They thought that he should know much better. He should realize how contagious hateful statements can really be. No wonder that many found it extremely worrisome how Bolsonaro was legitimizing what others would only dare to say in their kitchens and bedrooms. What's quite telling about the way people received his messages is that after his election, one journalist wrote:

No one has better leveraged hatred, fear and frustration than Bolsonaro. He has done so especially among sections of the white middle-class, who have suffered the erosion of their buying power and watched as the black community refused to return to its historical subaltern position. And especially among men challenged by women who decried sexual harassment and misogynistic jokes. Perceiving that its cultural, racial and class privileges were threatened, a slice of Brazilian society has sensed quicksand beneath its feet.

The price is being paid, in human lives and with Brazil being made into a global pariah, for this investment in hatred.

In his election victory speech last year, Bolsonaro promised "liberation from socialism, inverted values … and political correctness." His own advocacy of violence, including praise for torture and the assassination of opponents, is interpreted by his followers as "authenticity." He has spoken out against black people, indigenous people, women and the LGBTQ community along with his adversaries, all labeled "communists." Brazilians who had hidden their prejudices deep in the internet's sewers began displaying them in daylight and on social media like trophies. Bolsonaro, in power, had redeemed such people.[1]

The Many Dimensions of Hatred

Sadly enough, the story of Bolsonaro isn't really a fairy tale. It is a very dark tale in a country where nobody lives happily ever after. Like the story of King Drum, it is a tale of the darker side of leadership. It tells how low people will stoop to attain a position of leadership. It demonstrates the kinds of levers they're willing to use to get people under their spell. And in the case of Bolsonaro, it appears that hatred became his chosen instrument—a weapon found in many other fairy tales.

In fact, as can be inferred from many fairy tales, hatred is one of the most powerful human emotions. And as long as human beings have been around, hatred has always been a source of sorrow and suffering. But in spite of the misery brought on by hatred, for some people it seems to be their driving force. In fact, there is no other faculty of human nature as persistent and universal as hatred.

We often hate because we fear people who are different from us. Might our fear of the unknown, our ignorance of the other, push us to take refuge in hatred? William Shakespeare possibly thought so, writing in *Anthony and Cleopatra*: "In time we hate that which we often fear." Perhaps when we hate

---

[1] Eliane Brum, *The Guardian*, 3 June 2020.

someone or something it is actually because we are afraid. And are we afraid because we feel helpless?

Love and hate seem to be very closely related. But if we take a hard look at both emotions, hatred is so much easier to generate than love—and much harder to get rid of. Here it's important to recognize that hatred is not necessarily the direct opposite of love. Of course, there is a connection, but it is a rather a complicated one. It is more accurate to say that the opposite of love would be indifference, that is, we no longer care what happens to whomever or whatever bothers us. Whatever strong feelings we might have had toward someone, they have dissipated.

Anger

There is also a difference between hatred and anger. Often, people who express anger feel sorry for their angry outbursts. But that can't be said about hatred. Angry people hope that the person they're angry at can be influenced. They may even hope that something will change for the better within the relationship. But with hatred, there is no wish for change. People who hate want to get rid of the object of their hatred. To put it simply, we get angry at someone because of what they have done or said, but we hate someone because of what they represent.

We can also look at anger in terms of behavior. We are angry because we consider a specific action of a certain person or group of people as immoral, unfair, or unjust. At the same time, we tell ourselves: "If only these people would be prepared to change their behavior, I would be willing to let go of my anger." Taking this factor into consideration, in some circumstances, anger can be useful and contribute to reconciliation. But before this happens, we would like the person we're angry with to apologize, to make amends. The same thing can't be said for hatred. With hatred, we are stuck. We have no hope for change. Not even a temporary change in behavior will diminish the intensity of our hatred for someone else. Instead, we see the object of our enmity as unchangeable, irredeemable, and unimprovable. The goal of hatred is annihilation, not reconciliation.

Contempt

Sometimes, we are repeatedly angry with someone and, if nothing changes, our anger may turn into contempt. We may decide that someone is no longer worth our anger and, in trying to regulate our anger, distance ourselves from the person who makes us angry. It makes contempt a cold version of hatred. As the philosopher Arthur Schopenhauer would put it, "[h]atred is an affair of the heart; contempt that of the head." Strange as it may sound, it could be argued that it is worse to be the object of contempt than the object of hatred. At least, with hatred, we are engaged, not indifferent.

Hatred Is a Hungry Beast

A little hatred goes a long, long way and being full of hatred can be exhausting. Hatred is a hungry beast that demands to be fed. Unfortunately, the more you feed it, the hungrier it gets. It's never satisfied. It feeds on your heart and pollutes your mind and will squeeze all that's human out of you. Hatred hungers for revenge and thrives on division and violence. It forces you to focus on animosity. It occupies your mind completely. And this beast can be so all-absorbing that it leaves no room for anything else. It leads to the emergence of demagogues and populist leaders. No wonder that hatred is the source of much of the violence we see around us and the primary fuel for war. Paradoxically, during times of war, hatred can become almost respectable, masquerading as patriotism.

Acts of hatred are often the easiest way out of emotional quagmires. Compassion for others requires much more courage. Look at Bolsonaro, the subject of the devastating profile quoted at the beginning of this chapter. Does he love anybody but himself? Does he know what compassion is? And very much like King Drum (alias Donald Trump), he stirs up hatred and thrives on divisiveness. Although he is the leader of the country, he makes no effort to unite his people—quite the opposite. He wallows in self-righteousness. In fact, in many ways he is a pitiful figure. He doesn't realize that building bridges is much more constructive than building walls. He doesn't seem to understand that hatred is an uncontrollable fire. If it burns for too long, it will consume him. But perhaps his passionate hatred gives a modicum of meaning and purpose to what would otherwise be an empty existence. His motto seems to be: I hate, thus I exist.

The Danger of Self-Righteousness

Isn't it strange that human beings can hate people they don't even know? Bolsonaro seems to make negative assumptions about people he doesn't even know. He is always ready with flippant, negative moral judgments. Without producing the slightest grain of evidence, he labels whoever is the target of his hatred as bad, dirty, dangerous, or all of the above. He brings out the worst in himself and any others who are willing to listen to his toxic talk. And he is not a lone figure in our present-day world. The same could be said for other political leaders in very different countries: Donald Trump in the USA, Recip Tayyip Erdogan in Turkey, Rodrigo Duterte of the Philippines, Viktor Orban in Hungary, Vladimir Putin in Russia, and Alexander Lukashenko in Belarus receive the most media attention but are sadly enough not the only examples.

We tend to resort to hatred when we perceive another person's behavior as unjustified and unfair (making us angry) or morally inferior (making us contemptuous). This explains why we often have a sense of high-mindedness when we talk about our hatred. Is there anything that contributes more to destructive feelings than moral indignation? We can all see that hatred is often acted out under the guise of virtue.

Bolsonaro, for example, believes that he is morally justified in behaving the way he does. He sees whoever or whatever is caught in the spotlight of his hatred as negative, immoral, or even evil. And what makes the world in which people like Bolsonaro live so tragic is that their motivation to hate is not merely to hurt, but ultimately to eliminate or to destroy whatever or whomever they hate, either mentally (through humiliation or revenge), socially (by excluding or ignoring people), or physically (wanting to kill or torment the targets of their hatred). Basically, people who hate want the perceived wrongdoers to suffer.

Green with Envy

A paradox for people who hate is that they can develop a kind of co-dependency with the targets of their hatred. People like Bolsonaro need "others" to give purpose to an otherwise empty existence. The "others" are needed to shore up their vulnerable identity. They seem to live under the strange illusion that their release from the pain of hating will only come when they make their perceived tormentors suffer. Of course, this is absurd.

Some people experience a simpler, more instrumental hatred that is based on envy, a basic human emotional experience that is deeply ingrained in our psyche, and common to us all. Envy makes us feel wanting and inferior. It is a rather complex, socially unacceptable emotion made up of a mix of anger and resentment, a very dark desire.

The root of envy is found in sibling rivalry, which can also be a basic source of hatred. Children are self-centered and, at that stage of life, each sibling wants full possession of the parent. Of course, this imagined state of paradise can never be attained. It is a desire that is going to be frustrated, and envy and hatred emerge as a consequence. The intensity of these feelings depends on the extent to which parents can contain them in the kind of holding environment they have created.

As an extension of these very early feelings, we may start hating another person or group because we envy what they have. But because envy is such a dark emotion, it's rarely talked about. We do not like to admit—even to ourselves—that we feel envious; that we hate another person for what he or she has.

An Infectious Disease

Hatred can also be compared to an infectious disease that fuels divisiveness and polarization. Generally speaking, a culture of hatred has negative effects on people's emotional, psychological, and physical health—and a devastating social impact. It strips people of their humanity. It takes away their ability to show empathic concern for injustices done to others. It has always been a major precursor of terrorist acts, massacres, and even genocide. And although such acts can have multiple causes, hatred, born of ignorance, always underlies them all.

Beyond Shame and Guilt

Hatred desensitizes people of any guilt or shame they might feel about their prejudiced, negative behavior and actions. It removes moral restraints and dissolves conscience. And when people are full of hatred, they are more likely to do unconscionable things—particularly if they do them with others. In fact, as I mentioned in Chap. 1, group participation in terrible activities is a highly effective way to absolve any concerns of our conscience. Groups provide anonymity, and when everybody is assumed to be responsible, nobody feels really responsible.

All too often, history has shown us how hatred can be exploited to lead the people of an entire nation to commit unspeakable crimes against a particular racial, religious, political, or ideological group. An example is an incredibly shocking letter sent by Walter Mattner, an administrative officer in the SS, to his wife in September 1941:

> There's still something else I have to tell you. I was in fact also present at the enormous mass killings the day before yesterday. For the first truckload my hand trembled slightly when shooting, but one gets used to it. By the time the tenth truck arrived I was already aiming steadily and fired surely at the many women, children and infants. Bear in mind that I also have two babies at home, to whom these hordes would do the same, if not ten times worse. The death we gave them was a nice, short death. … Infants flew in a wide arch through the air and we blew them away while still in flight, before they then fell into the pit and the water. Let's get rid of this brood which has plunged the whole of Europe into war and is still mongering in America until it drags them into the war as well. Hitler's words are coming true, what he once said before the war began: if Jewry believes to be able to incite a war in Europe again, it won't be the Jews who'll triumph, but it will herald the end of Jewry in Europe.[2]

What Gets Split in Splitting?

What can explain the ability of a man like Mattner to murder the children of others while thinking of his own? The short answer is the defense mechanism of splitting (earlier referred to in Chap. 1), a process that also contributes to stereotyping.[3] It is probably accurate to say that stereotyping has been with us since the dawn of time. We can even consider it as part of our evolutionary heritage. For as long as *Homo sapiens* have walked the Earth, there have been in-groups and out-groups. There has always been the proclivity to split the world into friends and enemies. There have always been the "others."

From a psychological perspective, people who hate are more likely to use splitting as a defense mechanism. They think, feel, and behave from an in-group versus an out-group perspective. Resorting to these mental acrobatics makes the world more comprehensible. As I have mentioned before in describing the behavior of populist leaders, it is convenient to divide everything and everyone into friends and enemies; it creates a more simplified world of us versus them. Splitting is so much easier than trying to hold two thoughts about people in our heads at the same time.

---

[2] https://training.ehri-project.eu/sites/training.ehri-project.eu/files/Excerpts%20of%20letters%20from%20a%20police%20secretary%20in%20Mogilev%20to%20his%20wife%20EN.pdf.
[3] Otto F. Kernberg (1990). *Borderline Conditions and Pathological Narcissism*. New York: Aronson.

When splitting, the ins take the outs as the object of their wrath, blaming them for whatever they think is wrong with the world. To confirm their preconceived notions, they seek out facts selectively, confirming what they like to believe, resorting to what's known as confirmation bias, the tendency to search for, interpret, favor, and recall information that confirms or supports prior beliefs or values.[4] Mattner's letter is a horrendous example of these mental, dehumanizing acrobatics and incidentally reveals how extremely contagious they can be.

Populist demagogic leaders such as Bolsonaro successfully amplify prejudices that already exist, although they may seem dormant. And, as mentioned in Chap. 1, populist leaders claim to represent the unified will of the people, claiming that they are going to "drain the swamp" of corrupt practices.

People like Bolsonaro give their constituencies permission to say things that would previously have been taboo. By opening old wounds, they encourage the eruption of hatred and strip away whatever fragile layer of civility and civic decency might have existed. They not only weaken the rule of law, but they also weaken the social norms that enforce civic relationships. They are a danger to democratic systems and talented at creating pseudo-emergencies that justify destroying constitutional safeguards that could serve as a check on their power. The creation of burning platforms has always been a strategy for rallying troops to a cause.

Cultish Behavior

Demagogues like Bolsonaro are attractive to some because they attempt to elevate their constituencies by attacking and demonizing everyone else. They tell this selected group that they are special, or righteous. These tactics are a seductive way to make people identify with whatever the leader stands for—the tale of King Drum being another disturbing example.

They create conditions within their constituency that discourage any form of critical thinking. They have no tolerance for critical questions (the leader is always right), create paranoia about outsiders, and encourage their followers to subscribe to their ideologies. They reach a point where they can say or do the most outrageous things without losing the members of their fan club. And hatred generates more hatred until it becomes a cultural pattern, iterated by

---

[4] Clifford R. Mynatt, Michael E. Doherty, and Ryan Tweney (1977). Confirmation bias in a simulated research environment: An experimental study of scientific inference, *The Quarterly Journal of Experimental Psychology*. 29 (1), 85–95.

the noisy few who buy into it while the more level-headed, quiet but intimidated majority are reluctant to air their contradictory views in public.

But it is imperative to realize that silence is not the answer. It creates the illusion that everybody concurs with what's being said. When people claim that everyone thinks alike, it's likely that no one is thinking at all. Faced with hate speech, we should be brave enough to say that this is unacceptable. It is important to set boundaries for the behavior of leaders like Bolsonaro.

Demagogues feed on division the way a fire feeds on oxygen. They are the high priests of conspiracy theories, which, along with irrational beliefs and the proliferation of fake news, are phenomena enabled by technology. As already mentioned in Chap. 1, social media has ensured that hate-based rhetoric has found a powerful home, with many governing bodies now struggling with the problem of how to deal with it; how to encourage freedom of speech while creating fact-based interchanges. Frighteningly, Bolsonaro, his inner circle, and even his family, like those of other demagogues, are masters at manipulating social media and creating a world full of untruths and factoids, in which ethical, value-based behavior finds no place. As the Spanish philosopher Jose Ortega y Gasset observed sadly, "[h]atred … leads to the extinction of values."

What's Inside and What's Outside?

There are many reasons why we develop feelings of hatred or intense dislike. Interestingly enough, the things we hate about others may be the things we most dislike in ourselves. In general, we have a tendency to project on others unwanted parts of ourselves.[5] We don't want to see any badness within ourselves out of fear of being excluded by others. As social animals, once more referring to the discussion in Chap. 1, we are afraid of being ostracized, to be no longer part of a social group. So, while repressing the darker parts of ourselves, we project them onto others, to defend ourselves against this imagined threat. The people on whom we project our negativity become scapegoats. And through this projective mechanism, people who hate often try to maintain a very favorable image of themselves. However, their sense of self-esteem is very shaky. Therefore, when they come under any form of attack—when they feel threatened—they react violently toward those who perceive them negatively. For these people, a narcissistic injury is always around the corner and the flame of hatred can be lit at any time.

---

[5] George E. Vaillant (1992). *Ego Mechanisms of Defense: A Guide for Clinicians and Researchers*. Washington, DC: American Psychiatric Press.

Interpersonal Versus Intergroup Hatred

We should distinguish between interpersonal and intergroup hatred. In the case of the former, we can expect that recurrent experiences of humiliation, ridicule, or public shame by a partner or someone we have had dealings with will contribute to intense hatred toward whoever it is. In most instances—taking an interpersonal perspective—we hate people with whom we are familiar. We rarely direct intense emotions at people we don't know. A major reason why we experience hatred is usually some kind of betrayal—maybe infidelity but also any kind of broken promise—or an intense dislike of another person's personality. However, hatred toward a specific person may be redirected toward the group to which this person belongs. It is fair to say that intergroup hatred follows the pattern of interpersonal hatred and is characterized by the fear that the out-group might have a malicious intent.

When we feel threatened by perceived outsiders, we automatically turn toward our in-group—the people with whom we identify—as a survival mechanism. And sadly enough, nothing seems to bring people together as much as mutual hatred. Hatred has a tremendous bonding power. Thus, a loathed out-group that we imagine is attacking the interests of the group we have joined will make our in-group identity more salient. Furthermore, hating seems to be much easier if we imagine that the people in the out-group are all alike, while, paradoxically, common hatred will unite even the most heterogeneous elements of the in-group. Strangely enough, sharing negative opinions of other people has a stronger bonding power than sharing positive opinions.[6]

The perception of out-group homogeneity is an essential feature of this interpersonal process. It enables people who resort to splitting to generalize from the negative behavior of a single out-group member to a negative appraisal of the entire group. As mentioned previously, the world becomes so much simpler when it is seen in black and white, so that "love" for the in-group is paralleled by "hatred" for the out-group. The hatred evoked through this splitting process may give rise to a desire to take revenge and eventually eliminate the out-group. And populist, demagogic leaders know how to exploit this behavior pattern.

When we move from an interpersonal to an intergroup perspective, we no longer need to know the people we hate. It is enough to hate a group of people because of what they represent in our imagination (perhaps power, wealth,

---

[6] Jonathan R. Weaver and Jennifer Bosson (2011). I Feel Like I Know You: Sharing Negative Attitudes of Others Promotes Feelings of Familiarity, *Personality and Social Psychology Bulletin*. 37 (4), 481–491.

values, past behaviors, or identity). And sadly, what needs to be added, hate tends to spread further and faster when it's directed at a group, rather than at an individual. When we hate a group, the intensity of our hatred can grow without the controls of specificity or contradictory information, for example, the empathy or reappraisal of a person that can counter interpersonal hatred.

The Power of Ideology

Hatred at group level is often driven by ideology, some kind of belief system that promises a better future for all, the caveat being that this "paradise" can only be reached if the members of the out-group are no longer there to prevent it. This is something that populist leaders like Bolsonaro actively encourage. According to these ideologues, the only reason this promised land hasn't yet been achieved is due to the alleged (imaginary) nefarious activities of the members of this corrupt, evil out-group. This better world can only be attained by taking the out-group out of the equation. At the same time, whatever action these people undertake is legitimized by their ideology. Humankind has been subjected to the atrocious outcomes of such rationalization all too often.

A more straightforward reason for behaving the way they do may have something to do with the earlier mentioned emotion of envy. Often, people may be envious of the better socioeconomic conditions of the targeted out-group and simply want what the other group has. They justify the action they take against the out-group by assuring themselves that they have been exploited or oppressed by them.

Actually, from an evolutionary perspective, we can draw on another rationale for this kind of behavior. A common explanation for intergroup conflict could be that it provides benefits to individuals within groups in the form of reproduction-enhancing resources, such as food, territory, or mates. We could even argue that by depriving perceived rivals of their resources, the members of the in-group are increasing their chances of survival. This is the territorial imperative at work, the need to claim and defend a terrain.

Dehumanization

Populist demagogic leaders resort to a predictable playbook: everyone outside the in-group is rapidly labeled as subhuman. Walter Mattner's own words in the letter to his wife illustrate this dramatic dehumanization process. The facilitating factor enabling intergroup hatred is the dehumanization of individuals or groups. Being part of a group (racial, cultural, or other), we may have negative knee-jerk reactions to other people who we perceive as different from us. This is especially true if we have only minimal exposure to them. It is quite easy for human beings not to see others in their full humanity. By applying categorizations, images, and metaphors to dehumanized groups, people arrive at the same kinds of emotions they would normally apply to nonhuman agents that are the cause of damage and disease, and transfer the negative feelings triggered by "vermin" to whatever group that's under attack. Through these mental gymnastics, a kind of moral disengagement takes place, whereby people accept behavior toward "others" that they would, in other circumstances, recognize as immoral, unethical, and unfair. By characterizing "others" as unclean, or predatory, they carry over primitive feelings like disgust, anger, fear, and hatred. And as we saw in the example of Walter Mattner, these primary emotions are used to inspire and justify extreme measures against despised groups. Also, the perception of others as less than human appears to have a neurological impact, deactivating the empathy centers in the brain and any pangs of conscience people might have.[7] If the hater views the target of hatred as barely human or even subhuman, anything goes; every atrocity is allowed. Moral barriers have completely dissipated.

The act of designating a person or group of people as inferior is a key motivator of prejudice, discrimination, and oppression. Being part of a group that acts out atrocities provides a sense of anonymity. This combination of dehumanization and anonymity makes hideous acts easier. And as I have said before, with anonymity comes a lack of personal responsibility. This unholy union between anonymity and dehumanization lies at the source of terrorism, hate crimes, mass killings, and many other atrocities. This is what makes the behavior of leaders like Bolsonaro so dangerous.

A Learned Experience

We all have an inborn capacity for aggression as well as compassion. How these predispositions evolve as we grow up very much depends on the mindful choices made by individuals and families, and how they are expressed within the communities and cultures in which we live. How we end up very much depends on the socialization processes to which we are exposed. The reason why we hate appears to be the outcome of a complex interface between our psychological makeup, our family background, and our cultural and sociopolitical history. Clearly, in this process, parents, playmates, teachers, and the

---

[7] Jean Decety (2010). The Neurodevelopment of Empathy in Humans, *Developmental Neuroscience*. 32 (4), 257–267.

media of various kinds will play an important role. But as the first and principal caregivers, parents are the people most likely to plant seeds of hatred in their children. These seeds can flourish on a public scale when, as adults, these people attain positions of leadership.

The personal history that explains the reasons why demagogues find recourse in hatred can have many different causes, including difficult life conditions, past victimization, or a history of devaluation by another group. They might have grown up hearing collective narratives about traumatic experiences that the group with which they identify experienced from other groups. If their caretakers have been victims of violence—if they have experienced some kind of collective trauma—these emotional experiences are likely to be shared.[8] This kind of influencing process keeps memories of hatred alive from generation to generation. Accumulated group knowledge about the immoral and violent behavior of an out-group will affect how the victimized group evaluates these people now and in the future.

For this hatred to have been perpetuated there need never have been any form of personal interaction between the hater and the members of the hated group. But it is exactly this lack of direct interaction that can amplify hatred. In other words, the negative appraisal of the malicious character of the group will never be reappraised or contradicted by other information. Hatred directed toward individuals or groups is a way of distracting people from the more challenging and anxiety-prone task of finding out why they are so full of hatred. Hating is much easier than self-examination.

Creating and cultivating an enemy has always been an effective tactic to unite a group of people or a nation around a common objective and toward united action. For many leaders, it appears that the notion of not having enemies implies a lack of self-definition. Hating their enemies determines what they're all about. Letting go of the need for enemies would leave them without purpose. The alternative would be complete emptiness. Thus, these people will stubbornly hang on to their enemies in an effort to maintain and regulate their sense of self. The same observation can be made about their followers, who are caught in a similar psychological process. And, consciously or unconsciously, the leaders who lead them are aware of this. We can see how the processes of devaluation, discrimination, violence, and expressions of hatred toward an out-group help leaders like Bolsonaro enable their followers to identify with their behavior.

---

[8] Vamik Volcan (2020). *Large-Group Psychology: Racism, Who Are We Now? Societal Divisions and Narcissistic Leaders*. Quezon City: Phoenix Publishing House.

The Politics of Hatred

Given the powerful psychological impact of hatred, it is inevitable that it has always played an outsize role in the political sphere. As the case of Bolsonaro illustrates—and also the example of King Drum—many populist demagogic leaders use it as a highly effective, and simple, political tool to create greater in-group solidarity while, at the same time, encouraging out-group exclusion. We can all see how campaign ads, negative canvassing, and slogans based on collective hatred have become the bread and butter of many successful political campaigns. And, as I have said before, with the rise of social media, such activities have become even more appealing. Populist leaders like Bolsonaro have uncanny antennae that detect the worst instincts of humanity and know how to use the media to channel insecurity and hatred into mass political movements.

Psychological distress often becomes the spawning ground for these dreadful group dynamics. From an intergroup perspective, the sense of meaninglessness that stems from anxiety and uncertainty is also a key stimulator that motivates people to embrace such hateful activities. Distressing personal or societal events frequently undermine the way in which these people experience the world as meaningful. Consequently, to regain a sense of purpose, they are easily seduced by populist, demagogic leaders to have them adopt strong and clear-cut ideologies. It is like they are caught in a mass psychosis where their reality testing becomes impaired. The wish to believe even the most outlandish things becomes overwhelming.

All too often, in these situations, extremist belief systems become the main meaning-makers for people who have difficulty living in highly complex social environments. It helps them to make the world more comprehensible. Unfortunately, these people delude themselves into believing that they are supporting a worthwhile cause. Overconfidence in their ideological position makes for moral absolutes—another catalyst for negative action. Feeling morally superior, however, exacerbates a sense of intolerance toward others, adding to their belief that people with different values should be considered inferior.

We should really look at hatred as a mask covering a range of insecurities. When threatened, people with a fragile sense of identity are inclined to derogate others as a way of lifting themselves up, even for the most outrageous reasons. These contorted mental acrobatics are strengthened when others join the fray, and a structure of rituals, symbolism, and unique language is created, leading to cultlike behavior. Togetherness, combined with like-mindedness, turns into a kind of cocoon, the attraction of being together with people with similar (even if only imaginary) belief systems.

Social Media

As I have said repeatedly in this book of essays, the social media facilitate the creation and maintenance of these kinds of cocoons, and as things stand now, the combination of social media and hatred has become a great threat to humankind. It is now easier than ever before to blame certain racial groups or communities as the source of all evil. It takes very little, given the social contagion factor, for such accusations to strike a chord in the hearts of people who feel wronged, for whatever reason. Subsequently, a form of mass hysteria raises its ugly head.

On an individual basis, these people might feel insecure in their convictions; but encouraged by social media (and the added attractiveness of its anonymity) they are more likely to give voice to their hatred. And demagogues are very aware of this. They know how to weaponize social media, presenting themselves as saviors from a dystopian future that they are instigating themselves. Sadly, social networks have become ideal instruments for spreading negativity.

The internet has turned into the ideal incubator and amplifier for sharing and reinforcing extreme hatred. They have become an ideal outlet for very disturbing groupthink dynamics. Given the primacy of free speech, very little censorship is applied. Instead, the language of extremes is used to get people's attention. Leaders like Bolsonaro frequently juxtapose "the pure, innocent, hardworking people" and a "corrupt, evil, malicious elite." The message is that there is no need to accommodate other groups or factions or engage with them in the political order; nor is there need for prolonged discussions before certain decisions are made.

The key strategy of these populist, demagogic leaders the world over is to divide citizens against each other, and to blame minority groups for all sorts of problems. There is always a sense of righteousness in their communications, staking a claim to the high moral ground, confirming the dynamic of "it's us against them." Leaders like Bolsonaro keep their constituents' attention by perpetuating states of crisis, or even better creating pseudo-crises, positioning themselves as the "saviors" who will put things right. These crises have the additional advantage of diverting attention from their many shortcomings. Bolsonaro's efforts are a prime example of this strategy, fomenting these actual or artificial conflicts through the use of incendiary language that strengthens the "othering" of the people labeled as the enemy, whether domestic or external.

Most of Bolsonaro's messages are made up of negatives: anti-intellectual, anti-elite, anti-traditional politics. Looking at his personal history, "insult politics" has always been his forte. He tends to use short, simple slogans and direct language. And, like many similar leaders (Donald Trump to name the most famous among them), he engages in boorish behavior as a way of demonstrating his likeness to "real" people. Demagogues also like to assume anti-establishment postures, demonstrate contempt for mainstream politics, and portray themselves as the target of dark conspiracies. Their public remarks are full of factoids, based on fake information that frequently goes unchallenged or requires exhaustive fact-checking—results that emerge too late to expose falsehoods.

When populist leaders control much of the media, they try to exercise near-total control over the discourse relating to contentious issues. Journalists are ostracized, even imprisoned. As time goes by—as we have also seen in the fairy tale of the little Drum boy—these leaders create for themselves an "echo chamber" made up of influential sycophants who parrot the information they want to spread. Given the kind of political climate they create, they are likely to have delegitimized opposition groups, labeling them enemies of the people. Opposition politicians are either made ineffective through ridicule or intimidatory action or simply co-opted through promises of financial benefit or office. Like journalists, they may also be imprisoned, charged with fabricated offences.

As I have mentioned before, these demagogic leaders tend to be egotistical, self-absorbed, and confident in their own knowledge, having little need for consultation, deliberation, or expert advice. Many of them are flaming narcissists, with a touch of psychopathy thrown in.[9] Furthermore, unlikely though it may seem, they have very adaptable belief systems. Chameleon-like, they are ready to change their beliefs whenever it is in their personal interest. They claim to have the interests of their country and people at heart, but, in reality, they are merely looking out for number one.

Sometimes, these leaders reveal an alleged caring side. To reinforce their support base, they may offer schemes to help the less fortunate. But these popular interventions are motivated entirely by political considerations and are likely to be announced just as their "managed" elections are coming up. Generally, populist leaders are strong on rhetoric and weak on implementation; outside of activities that benefit them personally, they get very little done. Far from draining the swamp, as they may have promised when campaigning for high office, they turn out to be swamp creatures themselves.

---

[9] Manfred F. R. Kets de Vries (2020). *The CEO Whisperer: Meditations on Leadership, Life, and Human Nature*. London: Palgrave Macmillan.

Leading with Hatred

History has shown that many leaders find it much easier to unite people with common hatred than with common love but, unsurprisingly, people who lead with hatred don't get the best out of people. Throughout human history, the demagogue's formula for every atrocity has been to differentiate, divide, and destroy and once hatred is let loose, it is very difficult to keep it under control.

To get to where he is now, Bolsonaro unleashed an incendiary anti-establishment rhetoric that spread like wildfire on social media. Naturally, his populist statements found fertile ground with a legitimately angry part of the populace that felt left out and was fed up with the corruption practiced by the political establishment.

Within this context, like King Drum, Bolsonaro presented himself as the broom that would give Brazil the clean sweep it badly needed. He pretended to be a political outsider, raging against the establishment for its involvement in a string of scandals—yet he was anything but a political outsider. Before his election, he was an ineffective parliamentarian who never made an important contribution to the government. His main claim to fame had been to spark controversy and react theatrically when he couldn't get his way, to the point of caricature. Using his self-created, imaginary outsider status to his advantage, he cast himself as an anti-establishment, insurgent candidate with little concern for political correctness. Many disgruntled Brazilians were attracted to that message. His accession to high office reflected the country's fatigue with traditional politics.

And, as expected of demagogic leaders, Bolsonaro made people more susceptible to their "wish to believe." As mentioned before, people like to see what they want to see, in order to believe what they want to believe. We are biased to interpret evidence in ways consistent with our own desires. At times, reality and truth may be too much for our psychological well-being. It makes us want to throw such unwelcome information out the window. We like to be proven right and changing our view would be an admission that we were in the wrong, or at least had an incomplete understanding of an issue. Misinformation is especially likely to stick when it conforms to our preexisting religious, political, or social points of view.

With populist demagogic leaders like Bolsonaro, we can see how wishful thinking has gained the upper hand. It is sad to see how so many people have been fooled by his unrealistic fairy tales, which he never stops telling. In his presentations on the media, he goes to great lengths to make his followers feel good, even though what he says is far from the truth.

Very conveniently, many of Bolsonaro's followers seem to have forgotten that before he was chosen to lead the country, he was associated with generally illiberal causes. He was notorious for his misogynistic beliefs and his abuse of women, insulting a number of them publicly. His attacks on black people, gays, foreigners, and the country's indigenous communities were inflammatory. He even faced charges for inciting hate speech.

However, as mentioned previously, Bolsonaro knew how to take advantage of the economic crisis and attendant corruption scandals that had created serious political and economic instability in Brazil. Rising unemployment, in particular, proved to be a major vehicle for his rise to power. Predictably, many of those who had lost their jobs were attracted to his populist rhetoric with its strong racist, fascist, and misogynistic overtones. They were drawn to Bolsonaro's projection of himself as a strong, decisive leader, a common human response to feelings of helplessness. Given the many uncertainties in the country, they weren't overly concerned about the consequences of electing an authoritarian government.

Bolsonaro also appealed to the influential religious people among the population by persuading them that he possessed authentic, religious values. The reality has been quite the opposite, but it is sadly easy to fool people, especially if you are a populist opportunist with few beliefs and convictions, and all too ready to swing in whatever direction serves your personal interests.

There were skeptics, of course, and they were right in predicting that far from safeguarding the country's civic culture, Bolsonaro would do exactly the opposite. As a blatant autocrat, he would represent a real threat to democracy, spending much of his energy on systematically dismantling the country's regulatory framework. To the great consternation of many within and outside the country, he has also furthered the deforestation of Brazil's unique rainforests. He has even maintained that global warming is a left-wing conspiracy. Cynics, however, claim that his reluctance to take measures against the destruction of the rainforest is self-preservation, as part of his core constituency includes illegal miners, squatters, loggers, and cattle ranchers.

Remarkably, there is nothing charismatic about Bolsonaro. He is a miserable debater: debates make him very uncomfortable, as he has so little to say, so he avoids them. He resorts instead to nonverbal theatrics, like posing as a cowboy to demonstrate how macho he is. However, as I mentioned before, he undeniably excels on social media, the space where he knows how (very much helped by his children) to assert himself. Social media mobilized his election campaign and has been the perfect platform for his trademark campaign sign, a hand folded into the shape of a gun. He has spread and amplified people's fear of Brazil's crime epidemic, for which his proposed solution was to ease existing gun laws and put more guns in the hands of citizens. Since taking office, he has encouraged the police to use even more lethal force and explicitly praised police death squads. Furthermore, a dark aspect of his personal history is revealed in the multiple ties he has with leaders of the country's paramilitary gangs and militias.

Equally worrying is that Brazil is facing a dramatic economic crisis, but it's clear that Bolsonaro understands very little about economics. He is in well over his head. Like we saw with King Drum, the complexities of real leadership are way beyond him. Furthermore, as Covid-19 began to rage through the country, his only response was: "I'm sorry, some people will die, they will die, that's life. You can't stop a car factory because of traffic deaths." Like King Drum, his refusal to acknowledge the seriousness of the global pandemic, his dismissal of medical advice, his deliberate flouting of health regulations while the death rate in Brazil reached incredible heights, and his willful encouragement of the destruction of the Brazilian rainforest have drawn national and international scorn and fury—yet he retains the support of a significant proportion of the population.

Overcoming Hatred

The key to overcoming hatred—ancient and generational grudges, the old idea of "an eye for an eye"—is education at home, at school, and within the community. People who have positive attachment experiences, who are shown love and affection and have their basic human needs taken care of as children, acquire greater awareness of the impact of their actions on others, and vice versa. Empathic responsiveness is the antidote to primitive defensive mechanisms such as projection, splitting, and scapegoating.

As suggested, hatred usually grows from deep-seated feelings of insecurity or a sense of victimization. People may feel threatened by economic insecurity or alienated by visible cultural changes, like immigration. As we can see over and over again, populist leaders take advantage of these fears and, with the unlimited access most of the world's population has to the internet, it is easy for people to connect with one another—haters rarely hate alone. Social media swiftly outruns the mechanisms to moderate and manage content, while the Dark Web cannot even be reached by them. It has always been difficult to negotiate between honest, fact-based reporting and perceived censorship. Unfortunately, in many countries—particularly in "managed" democracies and dictatorships—achieving a balance is simply a pipedream.

Diagnostics

Human emotions are extremely resilient. Instead of dissipating, unaddressed emotions build up and intensify over time. Bottled-up hatred can have physiological and mental repercussions. It triggers the release of stress hormones, which, over time, can have significant health implications. The more intense an emotion like hatred becomes, the more physically demanding it is to contain it. If you don't do anything about it, like the infamous genie, once it is out of the bottle, it is hard to get it back in.

Neutralizing hatred takes work. The first step—and it's a big one—is to recognize that hatred is a serious threat to personal, communal, and national well-being.[10] The danger signs are stereotyping, scapegoating, and dehumanizing behavior patterns. Therefore, it is important to be able to recognize hatred in yourself as well as in others, to have the courage to challenge your own and others' perceptions, and to ask whether you are being misled or fed misinformation.

Self-Examination

Hatred keeps making its presence known because it requires very little real effort, compared to the investment required to genuinely understand others. It is much easier to lash out than to work out why you want to do so. Thus, if you notice that you are taking refuge in primitive defensive thought processes, it is high time you ask yourself what the origins of these are.

It is important to try to recall the earliest time you experienced hatred toward a significant person or group of people and what caused it. You will need to make an effort to recognize the reasons why certain people or groups of people create discomfort. What is it about them that you find so disturbing? Your challenge is to figure out how unprocessed feelings inside you are projected onto people in an out-group. Hatred is often the result of a lack of understanding and ignorance about the other. But if you have the courage to take this stance, you may experience signs of familiarity and recognize parts of yourself—your thoughts, your automatic responses, your presumptions, your potential for aggression—in the behavior of others. As the writer Herman Hesse put it, "[i]f you hate a person, you hate something in him that is part of yourself. What isn't part of ourselves doesn't disturb us." If you can make

---

[10] Robert J. Sternberg (ed.) (2004). *The Psychology of Hate*. Washington, DC: The American Psychological Association.

these connections and acknowledge your vulnerability, it will be easier to respond to others with compassion and explore hatred through empathic discourse and understanding.

One of the reasons why people cling so stubbornly to their hates is because they might sense—not necessarily consciously—that once they let them go, they will be forced to deal with the pain inside them. And indeed, the price of no longer hating others may be loving yourself less. You will have to accept that things you don't like about yourself are also part of who you really are.

Communication and Empathy

Reaching out and communicating with others is critical to overcoming hatred. Usually, you hate some people because you have never made the effort to know what they're all about, and you will not find out what they're all about because you hate them. But your attitude will change dramatically when you get to know the other party. You may even discover that people you are close to turn out to be members of one of your demonized out-groups. When you use your capacity for empathy, you might find that hatred of others supersedes logic, obvious facts, and truths.[11]

A major component of hatred is the negation of intimacy. Intimacy involves closeness. We often maintain distance because we have made up our mind that others will repulse us. When you find yourself in this situation, it is time to take risks and look for rapprochement. You may feel your hatred is righteous, but it won't bring happiness.

Transcendence

Hatred is like a drug and it can be irresistible to the point that it takes over your life. But do you want this kind of dependency? A society's progress depends on the way we liberate ourselves from hatred. Clearly, demagogue leaders like Bolsonaro will never be the architects of an inclusive society. They are unlikely to ask themselves why they do what they do because whatever they do is all about them, about holding on to power whatever the cost. If they have to demonize people to get what they want, they will do so. They will be unable to go beyond their immediate self-interests.

---

[11] Manfred F. R. Kets de Vries (2022). *The Many Colors of Wisdom: Becoming a Reflective Leader*. New York: Wiley.

History has shown us that demagogic leaders have incited hatred against ethnic and religious minorities for centuries merely to consolidate power for themselves. But in this process, they destroy a society's tolerance and humanity and block a nation's progress toward freedom and democracy. In light of this tale of hatred, our challenge will be to dissent from the poverty of vision and absence of moral leadership represented by populists like Bolsonaro or the little Drum boy. Thus, if we learned anything from these tales, it would be that we need to be watchful in pushing back against the bigotry and intolerance of others: our way of life depends on that vigilance. It is our responsibility and duty to break down the walls that hatred can erect in society. However, as long as we insist on hanging on to our hate, the world will not know peace.

As this all-too-true pseudo fairy tale explains to us, we can choose between two possible worlds—one filled with hatred and division, the other a place where people care about their fellow human beings, the sort of place you would like your children and grandchildren to live in. Given this choice, wouldn't you prefer to stand on the side of kindness, goodness, compassion, empathy, and conscience? It should be a no-brainer.

Taking this reality-based, non-fairy tale as yet another example, it happens that some leaders seem to have "blockages" as far as their brains are concerned. A number of them may be so obsessed by the righteousness of their actions that nothing can get through to them. Stubbornly, they will stick to their opinions. Their "stuckness," however, reminds me of a story of a wise man who was often asked for advice:

> One day, a couple went to see this wise man in the hope that he could settle a dispute. Carefully, he listened to the husband's tale of woe, and then replied thoughtfully: "I think you're right."
>
> Next, it was the turn of the wife. She told him her version of the problem. And after a short time of reflection, the wise man said: "You're right."
>
> Exasperated, the wife of the wise man, who had been listening to the interchanges, went up to her husband and said: "Don't be ridiculous, how can they both be right?"
>
> To which the wise man responded: "You're right."

Clearly, the wise man was not going to be caught in the web of "splitting." Instead, perhaps not very subtly, he gave a master class in looking for a resolution. He recognized the easy descent toward hatred. He was not going "to do a Bolsonaro"; he was not going to be stuck. Instead, he tried to have the couple (and his wife) reflect on their situation. He had made an attempt to encourage them to reflect on the other person's perspective by telling them that everybody was right. He was helping to get them unstuck.

Continuing with our chronicles in the domain of leadership—keeping Bolsonaro's toxic leadership style in mind—the time has come to move on to another fairy tale, an account in which another form of "stuckness" is present, in this case, stubbornness. And, as we will see, being stubborn can be a good thing, but it can also be a bad thing. It all depends on how you will use it. And, like hatred, stubbornness is often the strength of the weak.

5

I Won't, Therefore I Am

Smallness of mind is the cause of stubbornness, and we do not credit readily what is beyond our view.
—François de la Rochefoucauld

Stubbornness is the strength of the weak.
—Johann Kaspar Lavater

In the olden days, in yet another country that was far, far away, there was a queen who was known by all her subjects for her stubbornness. All the citizens of the country were familiar with her mantra: "No, I won't, and you can't make me!" They all knew that once she had made up her mind, there was no way she would change it. But having a queen who always needed to be right made life very difficult for her counsellors, who struggled to get her to pay attention to other possibilities. But "my way or the highway" was her constant response to people with a different point of view. The queen was convinced, however, that her stubbornness had always been the secret to her success.

Although all was well in the land, the queen felt that the country was not living up to its full potential. Often, she dreamt of its glorious past when it had been the envy of all the neighboring countries. She was quite nostalgic about returning the country to its former splendor. But as things were now, the country was bound to a larger Federation. This lack of complete independence was a thorn in the queen's flesh. She felt—and many of her subjects agreed—that there were too many non-citizens having a say in decisions that affected the country's future. What's more, she believed—as there were now open borders—that too many immigrants had been flooding the country, making her citizens feel like strangers in their own land. The queen was convinced that all these non-citizens were taking advantage of the services that her country provided. Therefore, she felt it was high time for a change. Her country should become "unbound" and free from outside interference. If so, she believed, a glorious future would be waiting for them.

Haunted by dreams of past glory, the queen decided to endorse a poll of her people, asking them whether the country should once more stand on its own. Although she was eager to initiate a "divorce," she allowed herself to be persuaded that this was not a decision she could make on her own. She agreed, convinced that the decision would have more impact if it were supported by all her subjects. To ensure that she got the outcome she wanted, however, her closest advisers framed the question in such a way that her subjects were encouraged to believe that, once they left the Federation, pots of gold would be waiting at the end of every rainbow.

When the voting day came, the people voted the way the queen wanted. Now, her challenge was to arrange an amicable divorce from the other members of the Federation. She was confident that it would take very little effort.

But divorcing the Federation was easier said than done and proved to be much more difficult than the queen had ever imagined. The decision to separate her country from the others had opened an enormous can of worms. Belatedly, the queen's counsellors discovered that not enough preparatory work had been done to understand what a divorce from the Federation would really mean. Only now did they realize the intense web of interconnections between the various members.

The counsellors told the queen about the trouble they now found themselves in, but the queen didn't want to hear any of their objections. She was convinced that her decision had been the right one. Stubborn as she was, she told her advisers to get on with it, and to settle the divorce without delay. "Where there's a will, there's a way!" she asserted.

Soon after the queen's edict, one of her counsellors asked for an audience. He said: "Your majesty, in the past we have had a shared military force to protect our borders. As you know, its main task has always been to prevent wicked trolls from infiltrating our country and making mischief. But given our steep mountain ranges and impenetrable forests, it is impossible to guard the land all by ourselves. We have always needed the cooperation of other members of the Federation. Do you think we should still go ahead with the separation?" The queen rebutted that she would have none of it. "You are wrong. We can defend the country by ourselves. You'd better get on with it."

Soon after, a second counsellor requested an audience with the queen and told her: "Your majesty, before we decided to leave the Federation, we forgot an important detail. One of the reasons we decided to separate was to prevent foreigners from coming to our country. We thought they were just taking advantage of the many benefits our country provides. But a recent study has shown that these immigrants turn out to be our most entrepreneurial people. They have brought wealth to the country and created many new industries to the benefit of us all. If we separate, our supply of entrepreneurs will dry up. Should we still go ahead?" Again, the queen argued: "We are much better off alone. There's more than enough entrepreneurial talent among our own people."

A few days later, a third courtier asked for an audience with the queen. She said: "Your majesty, in the Federation we have always been the major producers of magic mushrooms. Our mushrooms are in great demand throughout the Federation. But when we leave, there will be borders and the other members of the Federation may look for different suppliers." The queen responded airily: "Don't worry, there are many rich markets beyond the Federation, and they have been waiting for us for years. We will be much better off going it alone. We will manage!" However, nobody was able to get the queen to explain how they were going to manage. And so the discussions went on and on, with counsellors coming and going, asking the queen's advice about what to do. But her response was always the same, whatever facts and fears they presented: "We will manage!"

As time went by, and the divorce grew imminent, the queen's counsellors realized that leaving the Federation was going to be a major disaster. The divorce would be much costlier than anyone could have imagined. All wise economists had come to the same conclusion. Everybody in the kingdom would be worse off, especially the younger generation. The idea of recreating a glorious past when "free" was all but an illusion. Consequently, most of the counsellors had concluded that the best thing to do was to forget the divorce and admit that it had been a terrible mistake. The queen, however, refused to budge. She was unflinching in her belief that the decision to separate was the right one. In fits of anger, she lashed out at attempts to make her change her mind. It was clear to all that the queen perceived questioning the virtues of the divorce as a personal attack—akin to high treason. The few advisers who still had the nerve to tell her that the divorce was a disaster—implying that she was wrong—were dispatched to the Lord High Executioner, where it was off with their heads.

I will leave it to you to imagine how this story will end. My feeling is that, in this fairy tale, whatever the outcome, nobody is set to live happily ever after. It is a story of divisiveness and strife. Like the queen, many of us are set in our ways of thinking. We easily get stuck. We should realize, however, that a journey from "here I am" to "here I am" isn't going anywhere. We should also know that if we keep on fighting ourselves, we will always win, but it will be a pyrrhic victory. After all, there is no more perfect hell than being trapped inside our own mind. As the saying goes, if we are stuck in the past, we can only go forward in reverse.

The queen should understand that being stuck is not so much a circumstance as a choice. What could be helpful, however, is to look deep into herself to find the will and courage to change her mind, even if she finds it hard. But given her way of behaving, she appears to me like the mussel, a mollusk that has to make only one major existential decision in life—where it is going to settle down. After that decision is made, it will spend the rest of its life with its head cemented against a rock. The queen should take this story to heart. Does she want to be a victim of the mussel syndrome? To hang on to the past doesn't bode well for the future. She'd better realize that the greatest things in life tend to happen outside our comfort zones, not within them. Although our comfort zone may be comfortable, not much grows there. It is outside our comfort zone that things really happen. The queen and the people who would come after her had better keep that in mind.

What's Wrong with the Queen?

Stubbornness is a personality trait whereby people refuse to change their opinion about something or are unwilling to change their minds about a decision that they've made. As we all know, in most instances, to be labeled as being stubborn isn't viewed as a positive characteristic, the queen in the fairy tale being a good example. Ironically, however, one of the great paradoxes of leadership is that an effective leader often needs to be both stubborn and open-minded. In other words, leaders can be most effective if they stick to their vision—if they stay on course. But at the same time, while doing so, they also need to be open-minded. If required, they need to be willing to adapt whatever their course of action might be.

To put it another way, there are times when being somewhat hardheaded may have its advantages—when stubbornness can be a virtue. After all, leadership is about doing what we believe is right—even when there are a growing number of voices trying to convince us to accept what we know to be wrong. But whether what we're doing will turn out to be a virtue is often a question of hindsight. Naturally, when a stubborn person's way of looking at things turns out to be correct, it may be viewed positively. When we do not back down from challenges that could be labeled as positive stubbornness. In other words, there are going to be occasions when stubbornness is the way to go to overcome obstacles—to achieve great feats. Sometimes, only due to our stubbornness, important things will get done. It is stubbornness that helps us to accomplish our goals, come hellfire or high water. Thus, a degree of stubbornness can take us far in life, as long as our hardheadedness doesn't get the best of us.

In spite of its potential advantages, the synonyms given to stubborn behavior such as dogged insistence, intransigence, and pig-headedness doesn't make this quality very attractive. Very easily, stubbornness turns dysfunctional. To go one step further, there will be occasions when stubbornness will turn into a form of idiocy. In fact, angry stubbornness can become a weapon of destruction for both possessors and the people they turn their weapon upon. In other words, to be stubborn is not necessarily an asset. What may look like strength, in reality, can be the strength of the weak. Actually, stubbornness for stubbornness' sake demonstrates a high level of insecurity. Also, it shows an inability to look at whatever is happening from another person's perspective. Conversely, if we want to be effective in interpersonal relations, we need to have the ability to perceive issues through other people's eyes. If not, stubbornness may turn out to be a terrible character flaw.

Generally speaking, it appears that stubborn people fear change, even though they may not recognize that as being the case—once more, the fairy tale about the queen being a good case in point. For stubborn people, anything that doesn't fit their particular *Weltanschauung* invites resistance. Anyone who tries to impose a change in their routine or way of thinking is viewed as a threat to be avoided at all costs. It explains the dogmatic, rigid aspects of their personality. It also demonstrates—taking a developmental perspective— that these people seem to be "stuck" psychologically. Unfortunately, stubborn people are reluctant to accept that mental health depends to a large extent on the ability to accept and adapt to constantly changing circumstances.

Often, in the case of such stubborn people, it seems that the less they know, the more stubbornly they will stick to whatever they know. Stubbornness and ignorance never appear to be far apart. The capacity to make compromises isn't part of these people's DNA. Instead, they, like some of the leaders we have described in the previous chapters, also resort to primitive defense mechanisms, in particular, "splitting." Thus, all too often, they appear to be living in a world of stark colors, consisting of people who agree with their view of the world versus the ones who don't. Frequently, as we have seen with the other leaders described in these essays, for the stubborn, no middle road exists.

But only looking at situations in black and white doesn't make them very endearing. Frankly speaking, it makes them very difficult people to deal with. Given their psychological makeup, it will be hard, often even impossible, to have them change their mind.

In fact, as far as changing their mind is concerned, what these people especially don't like is to be forced to do anything against their will. Their basic motto (again, the queen being a prime example) is "No, I won't, and you can't make me." It seems that anyone who tries to change their mind, whatever it may be, will be perceived as a threat. Whenever there is a push for change, they will stand their ground. And given their psychological makeup, whenever there is some kind of disagreement about anything, they will be the last ones to compromise. Obviously, going through life with such an attitude doesn't make for harmonious relationships. And it is exactly their great inflexibility and rigidity that gets these people into trouble.

Given stubborn people's inflexible personality—their inability to admit that they could ever be wrong—they tend to shape reality as how they see fit. They'll make their points, provide evidence—selective as it may be to back up whatever they are arguing about—and stand their ground even if no one else will stand with them. In that respect, stubborn people are less likely to be prone to groupthink. They will not easily let a groupthink mentality affect them. And, as I mentioned earlier, the word compromise isn't part of their vocabulary. Thus, although at times, being persistent can be looked at as an admirable trait, to remain stubborn when the facts show that some form of change is required, becomes quite stupid.

An Attack on Their Inner Core

For stubborn people, it appears that disagreeing with the way they interpret the world is interpreted as a threat to their inner core. It can create a great amount of inner turmoil. It is as if it makes them feel diminished, humiliated, and considered as a not fully developed human being. No wonder that these stubborn people have a "No, I won't, and you can't make me" attitude to life. Their stubbornness becomes a weapon to be drawn whenever they believe that their way of looking at things becomes threatened. Any time that's the case, it brings up associations of losing their sense of dignity, pride, honor, and self-respect. It brings up feelings of being belittled, of being a lesser person. Apparently, what they hate most is to be perceived as a weakling. Not surprisingly, they associate any act of backing down (even if it means making concessions to reality) as an act of a loser. Their reasoning goes along the following lines: "If another person is right, she will be better than me. She will have triumphed over me. And if so, I will not be the person I image myself to be." Obviously, this way of reasoning is quite irrational. But, as we all know, very often, emotions trump reason. Consequently, these stubborn people forego whatever the reality happens to be to stubbornly embrace the error of their ways. They prefer to stay in their emotional comfort zone, even when doing so is painful. It makes them act in totally irrational ways.

What also plays a major role among stubborn people are the psychodynamics of power and submission. Many of our daily dealings with other people involve decision as to who will take the one-up or the one-down position. Frankly speaking, most of us don't like to be dominated, to be controlled. Most of us tend to resist when we think that we're being pushed around. These feelings worsen, however, for people with unresolved emotional issues—stubborn people being a good case in point. Not much is needed to have them go off the handle when they believe others are trying to control them. In fact, often they feel they are being controlled and dominated even when the other person—the alleged controller—is just trying to be informative.

Another reason for some people's stubbornness is their tendency to fiercely hold on to their grudges. These individuals may refuse to let go due to some real or imagined insult or affront to their person. In fact, what should be a very innocent remark is quickly interpreted by them as a threat. Thus, these "injustice collectors" obstinately hold on to the big and small slights they believe they have been subjected to over the years. And, as can be imagined, when people have such an outlook to life, not much is needed to bring these grudges to the surface. Going through life with such an attitude, however, can turn their stubbornness into a sort of masochistic exercise. It becomes an invitation to suffer. But on a conscious level these people are unaware of the irrationality of their ways. It is why stubborn people are often unable to give a clear reason or explanation for their refusal to budge.

Furthermore, in an effort to support their way of interpreting the world, stubborn people tend to look for information in such a way that it has to confirm their prior beliefs or values. At the same time, they quickly disregard information that goes against these beliefs.[1] Clearly, as discussed in Chap. 4, they aren't strangers to confirmation bias. Naturally, by resorting to these kinds of mental acrobatics, these people believe what they want to believe. Illustrative of this behavior pattern is the fact that stubborn people will often only read the news from the sources that confirm their vision of the world. In

---

[1] Peter C. Wason (1960). On the failure to eliminate hypotheses in a conceptual task, *Quarterly Journal of Experimental Psychology*. 12 (3), pp. 129–140.

fact, they strongly dislike looking for other sources of information. Doing so would only create mental confusion. What's more, it could affect their sense of who they are, as their identity may have been built and sustained based on a deeply ingrained set of beliefs. But by behaving in this particular manner, these people end up isolating themselves within a reality bubble that only confirms their stereotype of how they wish the world should look. Consequently, they will not be open or discuss the possibility of any new information. Anything that doesn't fit their vision of reality will be discarded.

In fact, we can see how all too often, stubborn people do not resort to facts, figures, or scientific studies to support their vision of the world. Instead, to prove whatever they're trying to prove, they will use distracting strategies. For example, they are quite attracted to the "fallacy of the red herring"—in which an irrelevant topic will be introduced in an argument in order to divert the attention of the person with whom they are in disagreement from the original issue. Furthermore, when needed, stubborn people will use any other tactic to undermine their interlocutors. Anything goes when it concerns attacking the other person's credibility. They will even resort to insults or any other value judgments about people who disagree with them. It is exactly these actions that make discussions with these people so infuriating. All too frequently, disagreements slide into personal territory, taking on an *ad hominem* nature, thus being directed against the person rather than the rationale of an argument.

In addition, to further support their way of looking at the world, stubborn people prefer to surround themselves with individuals who think alike—another way of confirming them in their belief systems. People with different opinions are just too threatening. Thus, generally speaking, stubborn people go to great lengths to prevent challenges of their vision of the world. To them, everything that does not match their vision is quickly interpreted as a personal attack, thus necessitating a counterattack. It is what gives these people's behavior such a toxic quality. It is what makes these people so infuriating.

The Separation–Individuation Matrix

Naturally, the question that arises is why people turn out to be so stubborn. Why do some people become so fixated on their own ideas and opinions? Why are they so strongly resistant to change, especially when others explain to them that to change would be a better way to move forward? Why do they possess this "No, I won't, and you can't make me" attitude?

As has become clear by now, stubbornness tends to be a reaction to underlying emotional issues. It originates from a deep sense of personal insecurity.

In a way, it can be looked at as a maladaptive coping strategy to protect the core of the self. To disagree with such people will be interpreted as a negation of what these people think they stand for; it is like an attack on their identity. And as is the case with so many personality disturbances, the foundations of this kind of behavior are created quite early in life.

A number of explanations can be given for an individual's stubborn behavior. A rather simplistic explanation would be that some children may be motivated to display stubbornness when they discover that being stubborn is a good way to make their parents compliant. They have learned to use stubbornness as a tool to get what they want. And we can observe how "spoilt" children often behave in this manner. Of course, it is to be expected that when children don't get what they want simply by asking, they try to find other ways to get their way, likely behaving in a stubborn manner. Consequently, if the parents aren't able to stop this kind of behavior, the child most likely will continue behaving in such a manner to get what's desired. Thus, we could interpret stubbornness as some kind of learned behavior that gradually becomes hardwired.

But there may be more that meets the eye than this rather simplistic explanation of stubbornness. We could ask ourselves what's happening under the surface. What's really going on? These considerations bring us to a scenario that's taking place at a deeper level. It pertains to what's happening under the surface. Often, the underlying cause of stubbornness is overcontrolling behavior by the caregivers. What's happening is that they're trying to make all the decisions that involve their children. But if that's the case, these children perceive this overcontrol as a threat to their existence. They feel like they are being "invaded," not being allowed to express their true self. Consequently, their stubbornness turns into a defensive reaction to avoid the discomfort of being controlled by others—to protect their sense of self. It is like a cry for separation and individuation. They want to be an individual in their own right.

To further explain the early beginnings of stubborn behavior—to take a deeper dive—we need to pay attention to the separation–individuation developmental matrix that all of us experience. To be more precise, separation–individuation is the name given to the process by which internal maps of the self and of others are formed. These experiential maps, or "internal representations," are built up through interactions with the caregivers, and evolve into both positive and negative experiences within a relationship. Thus, during this important early developmental stage, innate elements of personality as well as the experiences of a person's life—if the process is taking place more or less successfully—become integrated. If the parenting is done in a "good enough" manner, the child will acquire a well-functioning, stable sense of self that can tolerate fluctuating emotional states within the self and with others.[2] Furthermore, the child comes to understand that the caregivers possess a separate identity—that they are truly separate individuals. No longer are child–parent relationships of a symbiotic nature.

Therefore, during this early phase of life, in situations when the parenting is "good enough," stable internalization takes place that creates a sense of inner security.[3] As a result, the child no longer feels anxious when the caregivers are absent. Helped by these internal representations, separation fears are less prominent. However, in situations where the separation–individuation process hasn't occurred properly—where these internal representations aren't well established—the child lacks a sense of inner security. Anxious and avoidant attachment are the consequences.[4]

Babies and small children have a deep inner need to be close to their caregivers, but it is always a delicate dance. When caregivers are emotionally unavailable, the child learns to cope by suppressing the need to be close. The same observation can be made when the caregivers become too intrusive—when they don't give space to the developing child, contributing to these feelings of "invasion." To defend themselves against this "invasion," stubbornness may come to the fore. It's a defensive reaction used to avoid the discomfort of feeling controlled by others. It becomes a way of protecting these children's sense of self—a way of proving to themselves that they are persons in their own right. Consequently, later in life, every time they are reminded of the kind of parenting behavior that they had experienced in the past, they may go into stubborn overdrive.

Given their fears of being controlled, these people may even behave in a passive–aggressive manner when issues pertaining to control become troublesome. By sabotaging what they are expected to do, they express albeit in a quite subtle way their hidden feelings of anger about feeling controlled. Every time, they re-experience this feeling of being controlled, they are likely to slip into this passive–aggressive mode of resistance. As a matter of fact, it can be looked at as a form of cowardly aggression—this sly, unspoken refusal to cooperate—but it is experienced by the person in the one-down position as being powerful.

Of course, as I mentioned previously, there is always the possibility of a more positive outcome, in that the stubbornness of these children might be

---

[2] Margaret Mahler, Fred Pine, and Annie Bergman (2008). *The Psychological Birth of the Human Infant: Symbiosis and Individuation.* New York: Basic Books.
[3] Donald W. Winnicott (1973). *The Child, the Family, and the Outside World.* New York: Penguin.
[4] John Bowlby (1988). *A Secure Base.* New York: Basic Books.

transformed into perseverance, meaning that they're able to let go, but will not give up. They have found the right balance. And as I have suggested, in a leadership setting, such perseverance can really pay off. Leaders who hang in against all odds can have remarkable results.

In fact, a prime example of a person possessing a modicum of positive stubbornness is Steve Jobs of Apple. From what we have learned about him, listening to other people was never part of his DNA. In his case, however, what could have ended disastrously had more of a happy ending. His stubbornness took a turn for the better. At the same time, we could hypothesize that this behavior pattern may have also contributed to Jobs' premature death.

Against all odds, Jobs stuck to the notion that everyone would like to have a computer in their home, at a time when large data-processing machines were very much in vogue. But he managed to will his personal vision of technology's future into reality, making fools of everyone who regarded his vision as madness. His stubbornness, however, made him also lose the company that he co-founded—something that could have been easily avoided if he would have been able to compromise. Of course, one of the great surprises was that he managed to regain control over Apple. At the same time, his stubbornness may have contributed to his early death. While diagnosed with pancreatic cancer, he refused conventional treatment for a long time, being a great advocate of alternative forms of medicine.

Jobs' stubbornness gave the world a wide array of personal computing and mobile devices that otherwise would not have come about so early. Therefore, in more than one way, his story has been a moral tale that stubbornness can be a good thing if it helps a person get the most out of life. Conversely, stubbornness can become a really bad thing if it prevents a person from living and experiencing a full life.

Ways of Dealing with Stubborn People

As I have suggested in these essays repeatedly, basic personality traits develop early in life and become somewhat hardwired over time. But this hardwiring makes changing people's behavior so difficult. Unless there is a considerable amount of discomfort, in other words, pain, they will not be prepared to change. And if their behavior has an ego-syntonic quality—I am referring to the kinds of behaviors, values, and feelings that are in harmony with the individual's self-perception—there will not be enough pain. Consequently, they don't experience a need to change, a *sine qua non* for any change effort to be successful. And if they experience problems due to their unwillingness to change, most likely, they will blame whatever went wrong on others. Rarely, will they assume personal responsibility. On the contrary, most often, they will transfer what's on the inside to the outside. They will reframe whatever their dysfunctional ways may be, blaming others when things go wrong. As a result, they will keep on doing what they are doing in spite of any form of pushback. They will keep on relying on their maladaptive ways of dealing with conflictual situations.

In addition, their tendency—very similar to that of other dysfunctional leaders—to resort to the dichotomous thought process of "splitting" doesn't improve their way of dealing with others. Sadly enough, as I mentioned before, in the world they have created for themselves, the color gray seems to be non-existent. In short, their world isn't a place where compromise takes on a prominent role. On the contrary, it is a world where people can only be "right" or "wrong." And they want to make sure that they will always be "right." To go one step further, it often looks like some of these stubborn people will even choose to be wrong just to prove they're always right.

Sadly enough, there's no one as blind as those who will not listen. And it is their blindness to their behavior that makes it so extremely hard to help these people. But help is needed as continuing in their stubborn ways makes life very difficult for them. It becomes a highly stressful way of living as the slightest thing can put them off. Everything that moves away, even minimally, from their conception of how the world should be, can result in a long-winded series of arguments. For these people, everything that goes against their view of the world seems to be worth arguing about. Any change in their *Weltanschauung* will be perceived as a danger as it would get them out of their comfort zone. They need to be "right," whatever the price may be. It is exactly this closedmindedness and inflexibility that makes stubborn people so difficult to deal with. It makes interaction with them so exhausting.

Knowing what we do about origins, in helping these people to change, we should take into consideration that behind this "fortress" of stubbornness, there is a great amount of insecurity. As a starter, we should understand that their psychic equilibrium will be quite delicate. Getting out of their comfort zone will be very threatening for these people. Any time they think that could be the case, they will resort to their default pattern which is to start arguing—something they have perfected while growing up. In spite of all their protestations, however, until they accept that things are not black and white—that most of what happens in life tends to be more nuanced—the healing process cannot really begin.

In trying to help these stubborn people, what should always be kept at the top of one's mind is that they hate feeling controlled. Therefore, in interacting with them, it is of essence to prevent them from having this feeling. At the same time, if the objective is to change their behavior, we need to address what's happening under the surface, but without coming across as intrusive and controlling. Thus, to be empathic—difficult as it may—will be important to establishing a working alliance.[5] Trying to understand why these stubborn people behave the way they do will be a great first step forward toward engaging in a productive, developmental dialogue. It is the way to build a working relationship.

In trying to help these people change, what should also be kept in mind is that stubbornness is a defensive response that will be activated when these people believe that certain ideas challenge what they think they stand for. In other words, it is activated when they believe that their sense of self is being threatened. Thus, the last thing to do in working with them is to be transformed (in their imagination) into a controlling parental figure who has been responsible for their problems with self-esteem.

Consequently, in dealing with these people, any interaction needs to be done with great delicacy. Thus, in helping them change, given their prickliness, we need to engage in some kind of "emotional judo."[6] Here, I'm referring to a process whereby we are not exerting much force of our own but using the force of our "opponent" to create movement. We need to help these people uncover and grow their own motivation to change. Naturally, to enable this process, we have to start with the assumption that these people will be able to solve their own problems. Again, to help them to get to this point requires being empathic—difficult as this may be at times. We need to convey to these stubborn people that we understand their perspective, that we accept their situation. What's of essence is to approach these people in a nonjudgmental and noncritical way. If not, their defenses will go up quite quickly.

Moreover, while discussing their situation, we should try to practice the process of reflective listening. In other words, we should make an effort to restate what we've heard them to have said and to ask questions to prompt the conversation along. But when these stubborn people say something that demonstrates a discrepancy between their goals or values, and their behaviors, we could look at it as an opportunity to point this out to them. Pointing out these discrepancies will create a degree of cognitive dissonance, thereby creating discomfort which these stubborn people may want to resolve. At the same time, it offers both parties an opportunity to look at future scenarios—how things can turn out for the better.

---

[5] Manfred F. R. Kets de Vries (2020). *The CEO Whisperer: Meditations on Leaders, Life and Change.* London: Palgrave Macmillan.
[6] William Miller and Stephen Rollnick (2002). *Motivational Interviewing: Preparing People for Change* (2nd ed.). New York: Guilford Press.

Going through this interpersonal process will enhance the stubborn person's ability to become more familiar with what desirable behavior will look like. As a matter of fact, due to the process of cognitive dissonance, a degree of doubt about the way they're looking at the world might be introduced, albeit in a very subtle way. It will be up to these stubborn people, however, to conclude that their *Weltanschauung* is not the way to go forward. But while going through this interactive process, given their concerns about control, we should always keep in mind that to force something onto them doesn't work. Instead, by going through these mutual explorations, by digging deeper to discover the origins of their behavior, both parties will get greater clarity about the real reasons behind their stubbornness. It will make our future interactions so much easier.

Clearly, at any time, during these dialogues, we should avoid any form of direct confrontation. Getting into arguments should be prevented at all costs. Instead, we should move the conversation along to where the stubborn person wants to go. It's essential to roll with resistance. Here is where the idea of the emotional judo part comes into the picture. We should never put too much pressure on stubborn people to help them change. On the contrary, we should empathically and respectfully discuss their opinions. We should allow stubborn people to verbalize their resistance to change. We should allow them to share their concerns or challenges. We should show acceptance of their behavior, even if it is not positive or indicative of progress toward desired goals.

What I am emphasizing is that it is of great importance that these stubborn people shouldn't see whoever is trying to help them to change as an adversary or a person who wants to destabilize them. To get locked in a battle of wills that will have no possible winner isn't the answer. We need to abandon the desire to win whatever the argument. Like it or not, if we want the other person to be open to our ideas, we must also be open to theirs, however crazy or illogical these may seem. Consequently, in dealing with them, it is important to avoid phrases like "You're wrong" or "You're not right" because that will only make these stubborn people go on the defensive. Most likely, from that moment on, any rational discussion will be impossible. We need to accept that these stubborn people may suffer from a "temporary hearing loss." Often, the only opinion they are willing to hear will be their own.

During these interactions, it will be important to focus on the issue, and not to take whatever the disagreements may be to a personal level. We shouldn't let ourselves be "baited," which is quite likely when stubborn people run out of reasons to explain why they're doing what they're doing. If they find themselves in such a situation, they will try to take the discussion to a more personal level. To avoid being led there is going to be important, because at that point both parties will be "losing." Again, behaving in this manner means giving up the tempting idea that we must "win" whatever the argument would be. In fact, in discussions with these people, to really "win" is to learn something new or explore another point of view. Thus, if we enter our discussions with such an outlook, this change of mentality will be reflected in our attitude. And it will make the discussion flow more easily.

When in discussions with these people, we may find that their stubbornness continually overrides common sense, regardless of the logic of whatever the argument is. In such cases, the best way to create doubt may be to encourage them to go ahead in doing what they think is right. Even though it may seem like a Machiavellian move, quite often what a discussion might fail to resolve could be solved quite nicely by a somewhat self-destructive move.

Furthermore, even when it appears that these people are regressing—that things are turning out for the worse—we should always try to be positive. As far as these people are concerned, to take on a cheerleader role will be important. We need to show confidence in these people's sense of self-efficacy—to identify their strengths. We should make them aware of their positive qualities, to encourage their belief in their ability to change. In other words, we should affirm these people's successes and achievements even though these might be quite small.

Thus, while trying to help stubborn people to change, we should always remind ourselves of the positive sides of stubbornness. As illustrated by the case of Steve Jobs, many of the people who made a difference in the world were stubborn people who were determined to make their dreams come true. Their obstinacy ended up having a positive side. Taking this outlook will be helpful in seeing the stubborn person as someone much richer and more complex than we initially may be inclined to do. It allows us to escape the labels and stereotypes that we often attach to these people. Consequently, in our interactions with them, we should always keep in mind that a bit of stubbornness, at times, can be a good thing. At the same time, however, we should help truly stubborn people to be flexible enough to change their position—to have the necessary intellectual humility to question their own ideas.

We need to make stubborn people understand, however, that their behavior will only be effective to a degree. We have to help them to stay open to new possibilities—to be able to admit when they're wrong. Thus, if we can make a stubborn person's issues conscious and keep them in focus, we have a good chance of bringing them into a better space—of helping them to overcome the suffering that it can bring on.

* * *

I'll end this discussion of stubbornness that started with a fairy tale with another fairy tale that the stubborn queen described at the beginning of this chapter could learn something from, given her desperate need—against all logic—to have a "divorce." Again, this fairy tale will start with "once upon a time."

> Once upon a time there was an old man who realized that his time had come but he was worried about what would happen after his death. Would his four sons stay together, or would they drift apart? He called all of them to his bedside, asking each of them to bring a stick with them. When they were all together, the old man bundled the four sticks together and asked each of his sons to break the bundle. None of them could do so. Then the old man took apart the bundle and broke each of the four sticks separately, one after the other. Turning to his sons, he said, "I wanted to show you that you are stronger together. Remember that when I am gone."

Turning back to my thinly disguised Brexit analogy of the stubborn queen and the powerful Federation—in my effort to mix fantasy and reality—let us consider this: does the queen fancy herself to be a major player, with a seat at the table that allows her to deal with large, influential countries like China, the US, the EU, or India? Is she obsessed by a glorious, but no longer relevant, past? Is she deluding herself? Having become a minor player, will she be ignored by these powerful countries and, most likely, not even be offered a seat at the table? That is a possibility worth considering. The question then is, will she—and the others who came after her with a similar *Weltanschauung*—be able to open their minds? Will they have the mental agility to face reality? Or will narcissistic self-interest blunt all reason?

Unfortunately, when it concerns narcissism and ideology, as we saw in the case of Brexit, reason often falls by the wayside. Reflecting on this sad fact, I sometimes wonder what the Roman statesman and philosopher Cicero had in mind when he said: "The wise are instructed by reason, average minds by experience, the stupid by necessity and the brute by instinct." It makes me wonder what's needed for leaders to be effective. And why is the world full of such toxic leaders? And what are the required qualities for effective leadership?

As it happened, walking in the woods around my house in the South of France, I was once again ruminating on the theme of effective leadership. At one point, sitting on the forest floor while contemplating the subject, I was struck by the work of a spider that was busily weaving its web. Studying the spider, I reminded myself (even though it sounds convoluted) that these insects, given the way they manage their webs, might be considered, at least symbolically, leaders in their own right. They teach us that destruction and renewal are essential for continued evolution—something that's also very true for leaders. And like these spiders weave their webs with the ultimate goal of catching food, leaders need to enable their organizations to become intricately woven groups of people within well-functioning teams that together can produce great results. Spiders, like leaders, need to draw on their strengths from which meaningful and transcending objectives can be accomplished. They're designers of meaning. By taking on this role, spiders turn into some kind of bard, druid, and sage, all rolled into one. It makes them a very creative force. Moreover, they're like the Moira, the three mythological goddesses, who while weaving the tapestry of our lives, control our Fate. Furthermore, seeing this spider in action, I was also reminded of the fact that spiders are remarkable figures of feminine energy—a factor all too often underestimated in the leadership domain.

Most importantly, however, when I saw this spider weaving, it made me realize once more that all of us must weave the web of our own life. All of us need to embrace our ideas and dreams. And as we build on our dreams, we also need to take action. We need to put the strands together that create our lives, implying that we need to make choices—the kinds of choices that fit what we're all about—that are in line with what we're good at. After all, the reality is ours to create. But having said all of this, perhaps the best thing to do is to have the spider talk for herself.

6

Life Lessons from the "Great Mother"

> *The spider's touch, how exquisitely fine!*
> *Feels at each thread, and lives along the line.*
> —Alexander Pope

> *Laws are like cobwebs, which may catch small flies, but let wasps and hornets break through.*
> —Jonathan Swift

Once upon a time, at the edge of a dark forest in a faraway land, there was a large pile of wood. But if you imagine it was nothing more than a pile of wood, how wrong you would be. For upon looking carefully, deep down in a quiet corner, beneath some dead branches, you would spy a little web, so small that upon first sight you could have easily missed it. But if you were to draw close, there it would be in all its glory—a very sturdy web, a masterpiece of engineering—a perfect structural design within the chaos of the forest. Yet, to see such a masterful design, you would need to pay attention.

Aided by the bit of light that penetrated into this corner of the woods, you would see the web hanging in there, dimly glimmering in the dark. Early in the morning many little drops of dew would be hanging from its silky strands, transforming it into a collage of diamonds brightly sparkling in the light. And although it would shimmer, you should not be fooled by its glitter. For while the web might look inviting, given its beauty, there would be an uncanny, deceiving quietness about it, the kind of quietness that's often experienced just before a storm—a quietness that makes it clear why perception isn't always reality, why things aren't always what they seem to be. The same could be said of this web. What you might think you saw would be very deceiving. It would be a web that could play tricks on you. How often have you been fooled by the strange interplay of light and darkness? How often have you thought you saw something accurately, but in reality, you didn't? In this little dark, unassuming corner of the woods, if you made an effort to look very closely, you would see, quietly hovering about, a black widow—oh, what a fearsome creature—the scourge of the insect world. Grandma black widow would inspire both wonderment and dread wherever she would spin her web.

* * *

Hanging in There

It was soon going to be bedtime at the web of this Grandma black widow spider. And she was extremely proud of her web. To her, her web was one of the wonders of the world. As a true master builder, it was Grandma's strong conviction that she had constructed a web like no other. And though one would never say that she was among the modest types, she did have a point. She knew what she was capable of. As an outstanding weaver, she knew her self-worth. She knew what a great web looked like. There it was for all to see, this lacy, wondrously designed web of sticky silken threads—this marvel of complex, organic engineering.

Grandma had positioned her remarkable web quite strategically, close to the ground in a dark corner of the woodpile. And as she had the gift of foresight, she knew what her web was capable of. Not only was her web a thing of beauty, but given its ultimate purpose, it was also a grim instrument of death. And like the beauty and the beast, amid this juxtaposition of silk and poison, there was Grandma herself, hanging upside down, motionless, at the center of her web, waiting for insects to blunder in—to get tangled in its silky threads.

Some of you may think that such a sedentary life would be boring. But not to Grandma. She didn't mind it at all. She liked living in suspense. All her life, she had loved hanging by threads—watching for things to happen. And if you would ask her why she liked this life of just hanging about, her most likely response would be that it gave her an opportunity to think, that it helped her figure out what life was all about. If she was in a good mood, she might even add, being something of an amateur philosopher, that finding meaning had always been her overriding concern. And if you were not satisfied with this answer, but insisted upon her elaborating, her rather flippant response might be that life shouldn't just consist of chasing after things, that biding your time was so much better. Of course, if you knew Grandma well, you would know that she had always been a great believer in having things come to her—the "things" in this case being other insects. And if Grandma was in a really talkative mood, she might add that running after these things was nothing but a waste of time. They were just too fast. Instead, very quietly hanging in there, Grandma would wait for her prey to come to her on their own accord. After all, her patience was legendary.

A Slice of Life

All of a sudden, Grandma realized that she had spent too much time daydreaming. It was high time she came back to reality. It was going to be dark soon. And with night approaching, it bothered her that she was still a little bit hungry. She would really appreciate having a little snack. Her afternoon catch had not been what it should have been. From past experience, however, Grandma knew that other opportunities might come her way. Even though it may be late in the day, there were still enough flies, mosquitoes, grasshoppers, beetles, or caterpillars moving around. Surely, she would be lucky. Surely, one of them was going to make a mistake and fly into her web.

Just the thought of her next victim made Grandma salivate. In her mind's eye, she could see it now. With all these insects buzzing around, she had a strong premonition that soon something was going to happen. And sure enough, as if she had made a wish, a tiny grasshopper jumped into her web. Without making a move, Grandma watched the scene intensely, observing how the little insect was struggling and how it was trying to free itself. But all according to plan, the grasshopper became increasingly tangled up. Then, Grandma thought, now's the time! And she knew exactly what needed to be done. Having had so much practice, she had really perfected her technique of immobilizing her prey. When the grasshopper had calmed down, all tangled in the web, like a bolt of lightning, Grandma rushed onto it, and using her fangs, stung it with her venom, paralyzing it. Delighted with her catch, she now wrapped the little insect in her silky threads, turning it into a nice, small package.

Afterward, quite smugly, Grandma reflected on how pleased she was that her way of eating was so much more elegant in comparison to other insects.

Tearing and chewing at flesh had never been her cup of tea. Instead, her dining etiquette was so much more refined. Wasn't it strange that other insects hadn't adopted the same technique? Wasn't it a great idea to prepare your meal by wrapping up your prey into a nice bundle, putting your digestive juices into it, and liquefying its insides to create a mush? Afterward, the only thing left to do—when she had prepared the mush properly—was to suck the slurry right into her mouth. In a way, Grandma compared it to having a smoothie. Wasn't it so much more civilized, much less messy than the more conventional ways of eating? Besides, as thrifty as Grandma could be, she was quite pleased that very little of her food got spilled.

After Grandma had finished her snack, she felt so much better. Now, looking into the small pool of water beneath her web, she admiringly took in her features. Wasn't she gorgeous? Wasn't she a magnificent example of her species? Who couldn't but admire her shiny black color? Who wouldn't be intrigued by the reddish, hourglass-shaped markings on the central underside of her abdomen? Smugly, she thought, given her ravenous beauty, no male of her species could ever resist her. Knowing the seduction game to a tee, she had always attracted them like moths to a flame, and, over the years, she had learned how to pull the male strings with great skill.

While Grandma was busy admiring herself, she had almost forgotten that she wasn't alone. Playing the waiting game, just thinking about food and the meaning of life was one thing, but what about her job of babysitting her ten little girl spider grandchildren? It was such a pleasure to take care of these little ones she thought, and watching them play put a big smile on Grandma's face. It was so nice to see them growing up—to spend some time with them. It was all this togetherness that made them such a close-knit family.

How quickly these little ones learn, Grandma thought. Frankly speaking, they were sharp as a whip. And even though she had been teaching them about life, she was also learning so much from them. Once more, it reinforced her strong conviction of how much adults can learn from their grandchildren. Once more, smiling to herself, Grandma was sure that these little ones would go places.

Of course, the reason that Grandma's final meal of the day took place so late was because of these little ones. She would spend so much time with them. Taking care of them left her very little time to monitor her web. Too late did she realize that some of the bigger prey had managed to wiggle their way out. But how could she be on guard every second of the day with all these little ones running around? Weren't they a real handful? But then she thought, why complain? It was so nice to have them around.

What Happened to Grandpa?

Although the little spiders were having a good time crawling about in the leaves beneath her web, they also knew that it was soon time to go to bed. Trying to stall Grandma's foreseeable request to stop playing, one of the more venturesome ones crawled up to her and asked: "Could we stay up a little bit longer?" And then the little one added: "It's so hard to go to sleep when there is still some daylight left."

Grandma thought about the request for a second and said: "Very well, little ones, but promise that you won't move around too much. I have still a little bit of room left in my stomach, and you can see that there are quite a few mosquitoes in the air. Please, don't let them see you."

Glad that they could stay up a little bit longer, the ten little ones promised to be still.

But quietly sitting around for things to happen was not their cup of tea. The little spiders were far too restless; they didn't yet have the patience of Grandma. After some time had passed, one of the little spiders became impatient and said: "Please Grandma, can you tell us a story? Can you tell us some of the lessons that you have learned in life?"

As Grandma was in a good mood, she said: "Of course, isn't that what grandmothers are for? What would you like me to talk about?"

None of the little ones knew what to answer so they kept silent.

Shortly after, Grandma became impatient and said: "Ok, let me tell you what I will do. Since we are all females amongst ourselves, it may be a good idea to say something about the role of women in the world we live in. Perhaps, I should talk about male–female relationships. I could start by saying—in spite of appearances—that we females are the lucky ones. If truth be told, we are the stronger sex. I hope you make sense of what I am saying?"

Again, Grandma's question led to further silence. When nothing was forthcoming, she continued: "I guess, you don't. Maybe it will be helpful if I explain what I have in mind. Haven't you ever wondered why we have the nickname "black widow spider?"

Once more, a deadly silence followed. After a short pause, wondering what to say next, Grandma realized that in the spider web of facts, many a truth gets strangled. The little ones never seemed to have given it much thought. But she pulled herself together and said: "You should know that there is a very good reason for our nickname 'black widow.' As with so many things in life, it is all about sex. And you are now old enough to know that the males of our species are attracted to us. They like to get close to us. At the same time, you should accept the fact that these males are also somewhat scared of us. As females, we can make them quite uncomfortable."

"Oh, so you wonder why that's the case? To begin with the facts, one reason could be that we black widow spiders are so much bigger. Also, it could be because our venom is so much more powerful. You better keep these differences in mind when you are older. In my case, I had to find them out by myself. Of course, these males have also more fantasied concerns about us. At times, some of them find women hard to deal with in their imagination. But whatever is going through their minds, I can assure you, my little ones, these male spiders will be approaching you not too long from now. And when they do, be aware, because some of them will try to deprive you of a meal. Always keep in mind that life is more than just sex. Even though there is something to be said about instant gratification, you always need to plan for the future. You need to plan for continuity as men can be very fickle."

"Take your grandfather, for example. I still remember clearly how he was circling around my web. In hindsight, I assume that he had smelled me out. As you may know, our webs give out strong smells due to the things we eat. Therefore, our perfume can be very compelling. Given those smells, your Grandpa, sneaky in his approach, knew that I had just eaten. He imagined that telling me about my beautiful figure would make me forget that fact. But how wrong he was, the idiot! As I had a full stomach, this was not the time to be seduced."

"All of you should know that I like having my meals when the timing is right. And the time may have been right for your Grandpa but not yet for me. He imagined, as he kept on hanging in there, that he could take advantage of me. But your Grandma is anything but stupid. She is not the kind of spider to be easily taken advantage of. On the contrary, the school of hard knocks has taught me how to take good care of myself."

"Do you understand my little ones, what I am trying to tell you? As selfish as males can be, your Grandpa was trying to deprive me of a meal. But although it seemed like a good try, he was going to be out of luck. It was not going to happen. He didn't realize that we, female widow makers, can have the best of both worlds. As females, we are quite multidextrous. We can do many things at the same time. What I am trying to tell you is we can have sex and also have a meal."

"I knew at the time, not giving in to your Grandpa's flattery, that he would come back soon. There would be another opportunity to get together. I knew that what he saw as my mysterious femininity would be the thread that pulled him in. And of course, there was also the pull of my magnificent web. I hope you realize, my little ones, that Grandma can be extremely seductive if she wants to be. And I had a pretty good idea that he had fallen for me, that he wouldn't be able to control himself. He was going to come back and get tangled in my web."

"So, all you little ones, to cut a long story short, I let your grandfather wait until I was truly hungry. My credo has always been, 'when not hungry, why bother to have sex!' You should always wait till the time is right. And as you all know, we black widow spiders are experts at waiting. I have to show all of you how to stay motionless for a long time—until you are wooed. Actually, my behavior toward your Grandpa was exactly the way I would behave while waiting for a fly. Slowly but surely, I was drawing him closer into my web, pulling all my strings, sure as I was that when I had him in my web, he wouldn't be able to untangle himself."

"I told your Grandpa that I was sorry I couldn't see him before, but work had been murder. And as I expected, as he was completely infatuated with me, he was more than ready to accept my apologies. Then, I gave him a fake smile. I flattered him, telling him that he was the most handsome male spider I had ever seen. And, of course, he fell for it. Males can be so naïve! Males can be so easily fooled! Actually, without too much effort, you can make many of them believe almost anything. Clearly, whatever I said, it was good enough to seduce him. Whatever I did, your Grandpa lapped it all up. He fell for it completely."

"At the prime moment of our romantic intercourse, when he was satisfied, but still in my embrace, your Grandpa wanted to get out. He wanted to get free, as so many males wish to afterward. And for all I know, he may even have wanted to move on to the next spider. Can you imagine! So many males have the nerve. And believe me, I don't think your Grandpa was very different. Sometimes, it makes me wonder whether males can have meaningful relationships; whether male–female partnerships do have a future."

"But I can tell you that your Grandpa hadn't counted on what was going to happen next. Although he was trying to escape my embrace, I held him very tight, making sure that he wasn't going anywhere. Frankly speaking, to escape from my embrace and the web I had spun would have been a miracle. After a very short struggle, I gave him one of my venomous kisses. Actually, I have to admit, kind-hearted as I sometimes can be, I gave him first a little anesthetic. But when he lost it, I gave him a full dose of my venom, bound him with my silky threads, and sucked the vitals out of him. In a way, metaphorically speaking, I discarded his body after having consumed his heart."

"Do you think, little ones, that I'm cold-hearted? Do you think I should have kept your Grandpa around? Truth be spoken, I don't think so. He had done what needed to be done. After all, you little ones are the living proof of it. But as far as your Grandpa was concerned, I had to plan for the future. I had to eat. I needed to be able to lay my eggs. Also, I can tell you, not having spiders like your Grandpa around creates much fewer hassles. It makes life so much simpler. And if truth be told—to put it more vulgarly—he should have known not to fuck with me. Somehow, doing what I did was because I thought he deserved it. Given my previous experiences with males, he was most likely going to behave like all the others I have known. And don't people say, trick or treat? That's what he got. I tricked him after treating him. As female spiders, we give life, and we take life. All too often, as I have discovered the hard way, what seems like love turns out to be nothing but an illusion.[1] All I can say now is that both of us, for a short moment, had a good time."

The Feminine Mystique

"Frankly speaking, thinking a little bit more about it, your Grandpa was quite stupid. He should have recognized my warnings. After all, I do have this hourglass sign on my back, making it very clear that when you come close to me, you may find yourself quickly out of luck; in short, your time may be running out. So, little ones, now you know why your Grandpa is no longer around."

"Unfortunately, the males of our species do not always realize how resourceful females can be. They don't always recognize our shadowy side. They don't see; they don't observe. They don't realize that we females are complex beings. We embody so many things, be it creation and destruction, cunning, deception, intrigue, wisdom, patience, light, darkness, and even death. But it is difficult for most men to grasp all the complexities of the feminine mystique."

Then, Grandma said, "Now, you little ones, what did you make of my story?"

The first little one could hardly wait to put in a word. When Grandma nodded in her direction, encouraging her to speak, she blurred out: "You really taught us some lessons in relationship building; what partnerships are all about. Clearly, when you love someone completely, you should be willing to give it all, even if it means—like it was in the case with you and Grandpa—total sacrifice. You should be able to let go of selfish motives. You should be able to give yourself completely. Isn't that's what love is all about? Isn't that the way to create meaningful relationships?"

---

[1] Manfred F. R. Kets de Vries (2021). The triumph of hope over experience: Ten lessons to create better partner relationships, *INSEAD Working Papers*, 2021/13/EFE.

"Oh, little one, you are such a romantic. Also, you're quite naïve. But who knows, with the way you talk, it could very well be that you become an ideal wife," Grandma mumbled. "At the same time, you might also become quite disappointed if you plan to be merely an extension of the other sex. Remember, as a woman, it is important to have your own identity. And as I have been telling you repeatedly, you should always be a woman in your own right, especially in this day and age. Don't turn into an 'as if' personality, taking your values and positions from those to whom you are attached and with whom you identify—who, most likely, will be your partner."

"What you need in relationships is mature dependence, meaning the capacity to express your feelings about your needs, but also the ability to create space for yourself. Like in any mature relationship, you should ask yourself whether the other person has what it takes—the qualities you are really looking for. I am thinking of the kinds of qualities that you like your close friends to have. Also, don't forget to ask yourself whether you have interests in common—if there are activities you like to do together. These are always good indicators of whether a relationship will have promise for the future."

"True enough, your Grandpa gave all, anesthetized by the sirens of lust. But in any romantic relationship, you should always be aware of the '*coup de foudre*'—be careful of love at first sight. Sometimes, it turns into something of a psychotic experience: both parties only want to see what they like to see. After all, it is quite easy to fall in love with yourself. Therefore, it is important to always insert a dose of reality into what could otherwise turn into an emotional rollercoaster. And you should always be conscious of the kinds of qualities you want from the other."

"At the same time, you should keep in mind that being in a mature relationship can provide both of you with the opportunity for personal growth, if you allow it to happen, which I didn't. Frankly speaking, I didn't believe that your Grandpa had the capacity for real commitment. I felt that he wasn't emotionally mature enough. Even though I didn't express it, I was really asking myself whether he had the capacity to hang in there when the going would get tough. I also didn't think that we had shared interests—so important in making a relationship work. It's essential to be able to do things together."

The second little spider seemed to be inspired by her sister's comment about relationships, and added: "Isn't love very often like a spider's web? The more we try to get out of it, the more we may feel trapped. Aren't too many relationships just whimsical processes often beyond the realms of rationality, cultural pressures, or even our own conscious will, plans, or intentions? Why some relationships work out and others don't can be quite mystifying. Wasn't there a philosopher who once said: 'Marry, you regret it; don't marry, you regret it also?' In his case, I wonder whether he ever married. Given the tone in which he said what he did, I doubt it."

"The problem with many relationships is that we may have this sense of incompleteness, creating the false belief that the partner is going to complete us. But that's often not the case. And if that's not a problem in itself, there are also some people who have this obsession to 'fix' the other. They look at their partner as a 'project.' Frequently, the reason they behave in this manner is because, while growing up, one or more of the parents needed 'fixing.' They were behaving in destructive ways. No wonder that it becomes a problem that preoccupies them. But as I have seen all too often in these situations, such projects turn into 'mission impossible.' What happens instead is that the partners end up fighting a 'guerrilla war.'"

"I guess, you aren't a romantic like your sister. But I wonder where you learned all these things. You must have looked around at what happens in other webs," Grandma said. Then she added: "But should it be this way?"

Caught in a Web or Offering a "Room with a View"

This comment made the third little spider somewhat uncomfortable. She was making a major effort to organize her thoughts. There were so many ideas going through her mind. All of a sudden, however, she seemed to have an "aha moment" and she said: "Isn't it true that most relationships are a gamble? Isn't it sad that most males don't really understand females? Too often, they seem to have their signals crossed. Hasn't it been said that men are from Mars and women from Venus? Sometimes, it looks like the two sexes are living on very different planets. All too often, I have overheard that the common complaints in too many partnerships—why they don't work out—have to do with such issues as feeling unappreciated, being controlled by the other, experiencing a lack of intimacy, or trying to manage the flirtatious behavior of one of the partners. And then there are these irritations caused by a lack of fairness—meaning that one of the partners is doing most of the work and the other not pulling his or her weight. Of course, there are also situations whereby one partner is overly critical of the other—a form of dealing with each other that doesn't make for a good atmosphere. No wonder that all these kinds of misunderstandings can make life hell."

Grandma said: "Very true. Of course, it begs the question why male–female relationships always have to be so messy!"

The fourth little one said: "True enough, but don't we all, at times, speaking once more of relationships, have this lingering, insidious, and ambushed feeling of being threatened—of being caught in some kind of web? It seems to be quite difficult in many relationships to offer each other a 'room with a view'—to give each other sufficient space. Sometimes, relationships can be quite stifling. It makes me wonder why some people want to be in a relationship at all. Is the reason that they were fearful of not finding anyone? Were they compelled to act in haste? Could it be that by giving in to social pressure, some of them thought they'd better lock in a partner fast—any partner—the alternative being that one might end up alone, forever? But if that's the motivation, these individuals can instead end up feeling trapped."

"Listening to Grandma's story, I'd like to add that in the spider world, the female gender is of extraordinary importance. And hearing what happened to Grandpa, I can imagine that many males of other species, often perceive us, the female sex, not only in reality but also in fantasy, as fearful maternal figures. No wonder that they like to have a room with a view. In their imagination, we are like the Great Mothers of times gone by—this primordial image of the psyche. And such reactions are understandable. When the males were young and had to deal with their mothers, they would most likely have been ordered around. At this stage of their lives, the females might look formidable, while the males might feel very small. This internalized image of the mother can remain. This mother figure could give but also withhold; she could be good but also bad. What a confusing, intimidating figure a mother could be."

"Actually, isn't it a paradox? Males have this fear of females while they live in a self-created male-dominated world. In spite of the power males may have, whatever we do, many males seem to look at us—and this is not necessarily a conscious process—as a powerful symbol of captivity. And true enough, in particular as black widows, we have the power to ensnare our victims and restrict their freedom before we take their lives. Sex with a black widow can be truly deadly. This is in contrast to other creatures, where the situation is more of a metaphoric nature—where females can be threatening in the imagination."

Grandma said: "Interesting how much you seem to know about male–female relationships. It makes me wonder where and how you acquired all this knowledge. Anyhow, in spite of male efforts to the contrary, keep in mind—as I have said before—males are truly the weaker sex."

Understanding What's Happening Under the Surface

The fifth little spider, somewhat disturbed about the way the conversation was developing, said: "As spiders, do we have to use others, to have them shrivel up, and then discard them? Is it necessary to have relationships end up like this, even in marriage? From what I have seen looking at my parents, too often relationships go sour because we don't recognize the signals that we give to each other. I believe one of the reasons is that many of us have this fantasy that everyone thinks alike. But that's not true. Each of us thinks very differently. But perceiving the other like that only makes for mixed signals. We have to learn to appreciate how different we all are. Female and male spiders communicate differently and may assign separate meanings to the same words."

"Furthermore, we not only have to look out for manifest behavior, but we also have to figure out what's happening under the surface. As we all know, what you see isn't always what you get. Isn't it true that everybody is normal until you know them better? We need to figure out what the drivers are of the other—what the other is all about. We need to make sense of the subtle signals. And even if others are trying to tell us what they are all about, they may not even know themselves. The slogan 'know thyself' is imperative. But from what I have seen, most people have very little idea of what makes them 'tick.' But if we don't figure it out, we may be in for a great surprise. Grandma, just think how you surprised Grandpa! But who knows, with the correct interpretation, Grandpa might still be around today."

Then, the little one added quite flippantly: "Of course, a major lesson to be learned is that you better never mess around with a black widow!"

"Males can be so ignorant," was Grandma's rather cool response.

Examining Our Shadowy Side

The sixth little spider was more of a rambler, but nevertheless quite astute. She noted: "I'd like to elaborate on what has just been said. We black widows are often depicted as hiding the ultimate reality within the veils of illusion. Our webs show so much beauty, so much promise. But at the same time, they are quite illusionary—as Grandma made clear. They are also webs of deceit. It makes us weavers, symbols of cunning. The moral of it all is not to be fooled by appearances. Unfortunately, we all know how easily people are deceived when you tell them what they want to hear. Just think about the world we live in. All this flattery. All these fake smiles. But we also know that if you don't watch it, your life can get sucked out of you."

"Sometimes, like with our webs, without really noticing it, there is much danger out there. What I am trying to say—elaborating on the question of how well you know yourself—is that we all have a shadow side, that aspect of our personality that we deem unworthy or not likable and therefore try to reject or repress. But we shouldn't. In knowing ourselves—in being able to live an authentic life—we can draw important lessons from our darker parts. Yet going there requires vulnerability; it requires that we have the courage to allow these parts of us to come to light. We need to do so if we are ever to figure out what we are really about. But if we are brave enough to deal with our shadow side, it will help us to come to terms with these parts of our personality. That's what authenticity is all about. Of course, some of you might say that, as a black widow, being authentic will always remain a somewhat questionable proposition."

"Dear little one, what a complex observation. What a mind you have! You're very perceptive. You have the making of a psychologist. Without trying to be facetious, you seem to be wise before your time. You will go places," Grandma mumbled.

Life as a Darwinian "Soup"

The seventh little spider, somewhat in a philosophical mood, taking a different angle, said: "I would like to change the discussion. I would like to talk about different kinds of power relationships. What I have learned, watching Grandma, is that when some weak creature comes up against her web, there is a good chance that it will be caught. But that's not true for the big ones. Most likely, they will break through and get away. We may talk about equality in life, but, in reality, might is all too often right. Life is not always fair. Fair process is often hard to find. Of course, Grandma, I have heard you say 'Get used to it, be real, that's life!' But should it be this way? Too many don't deserve what they get, while many don't get what they deserve."

"You'd better accept these facts of life. It will give you a more realistic view of how to get ahead in this world. Life can be quite Darwinian," Grandma responded.

"Haven't we sometimes heard the expression 'being like a spider in the web,' referring to our ability to implement grand schemes and plans," the eighth little spider said. "I think to be a successful spider, to go anywhere in life, you'd better be somewhat of a schemer. Or to say it more plainly, you need to be somewhat of a Machiavellian. Even though it sounds very self-serving, to survive in this world of ours, you need to be focused on your own interests. In other words, to succeed—to be in a leadership position as a spider—there will be times when you have to manipulate, deceive, and exploit others to achieve your goals. That may be what's needed to get ahead. And just as in the case of Grandpa, you may also have to flatter, to lie, and to deceive when necessary, to get your way. To get where you want to be, you may have to come across as charming and confident. It is all part of the game. But whatever you do, you'd better not reveal your true intentions. And while you're planning, calculating how you can be on top of the web, you need to stay focused on your own ambitions."

"Furthermore, you'd better forget about empathy. Also, forget about compassion. And forget about having emotional attachments. These feelings will not get you anywhere. They will just lead you astray. Accept that you may have to cause others harm to achieve your ends. And as far as principles are concerned, what are those? Better be flexible, if you understand what I mean. Like it or not, there will be times when you need to let go of these principles. In that respect, we should thank Grandma for being such a great role model," the little spider ended her speech.

Grandma agreed: "You have to defend yourself. And you're correct about being somewhat of a Machiavellian to be successful. As spiders, you have to deal with what can be extremely tangled webs. There will be many times when you will find yourself in very knotty situations. Therefore, in order to run a successful web, do we need to forget about such leadership qualities as being humble, authentic, truthful, trustworthy, and selfless? Perhaps, it is much more effective to be deceitful, self-centered, greedy, and looking out for number one. Like it or not, are these the facts of life? Does it have to be this way? Is there a choice?"

The Seven Cs of Effective Leadership

The ninth little spider said: "I beg to disagree with the Darwinian option. I really wonder if you need to resort to such behavior to be successful as a spider. I realize that, compared to my sister, I may sound idealistic, but I don't like all this Machiavellianism. In my opinion, to be successful in running an effective web, it all comes down to seven key leadership qualities: Complexity, Confidence, Compassion, Care, Courage, Critical thinking, and Communication—which, for the sake of simplicity I like to refer to as the 7

Cs. Listening to Grandma's stories, I suggest that we should be looking for leaders who have the capacity to deal with *complexity*, in other words, who possess a long-term, systemic outlook in dealing with problems. I'm referring to those who are strategic thinkers. Such individuals are capable of becoming true merchants of hope and can become so with a vision grounded in a realistic assessment of things. Furthermore, I have come to realize how self-*confidence* stimulates curiosity and contributes to a greater open-mindedness. If your mindset is grounded in an inner sense of security, it will contribute to better decision-making. This confidence widens your perspective on new learning opportunities. Also, if you possess *compassion*, it will help you approach the people you lead with humility, respect, appreciation, and empathy. And trust—rather than distrust and conspiracy theories—will grow naturally. And this reflective capability and emotional intelligence further sustain such feelings of trust. In addition, a sense of compassion—strange as it may be for a black widow—may enable you to influence others. To have *compassion* will be an essential quality. Also, you need to *care* passionately about whatever you're doing. Passion and inspiration will go hand in hand. In addition, you need to have the *courage* of your convictions. You need to have personal integrity, moral values, and persistence to make tough decisions. Furthermore, I believe, to be truly successful in running a web, you need to become skilled in *critical thinking*. It will make you more effective in whatever you're doing. You need to be able to think things through fueled by a deep understanding of what you are doing, and why. Finally, to be like our grandma, you need to improve your *communication* skills—the ability to present your ideas concisely and coherently so that you can educate your children and grandchildren when the time comes."

Grandma said: "That's quite a mouthful. But I think that you may be a trifle too idealistic, at least for a black widow."

Searching for Meaning—Weaving the Web of Our Lives

The tenth little one was more hesitant about what to say. She was wondering how she could sum up many of the ideas that had come to the fore during the discussion. Listening to the others, her thoughts had been going all over the place. Finally, she managed to pull herself together, whispering to all: "Clearly, just as we spiders weave webs to make a living, so too, we have the responsibility to weave the web of our own life. And what I believe Grandma has been trying to tell us is that the web we weave can either serve us or enslave us. Our webs will be a reminder of the choices that we make to construct our lives.

Therefore, for each of us, the dilemma of choice is ever-present, particularly concerning love and work. And reluctant as we may be, it is up to us to make these choices wisely. We shouldn't be scared of doing so. Also, it is for all to see how destinies will cross paths in life's diverse web. Thus, we should be very mindful of our choices; we need to be smart about the life we weave for ourselves."

"And to be somewhat philosophical—to prescribe how to live a meaningful life—I can imagine that there are *five pillars of 'being'* that greatly influence the way we experience what's meaningful to each of us, what is important. To start with, meaning in life depends on a sense of *belonging*, implying the depth of our interpersonal relationships; it depends on our ability to bond with others, including our capacity for generativity—the willingness (when the time arrives) to nurture and guide the younger ones, thereby contributing to the next generation. Just look at how Grandma has been taking care of us, how she has bonded us together. Meaning also has something to do with the degree to which we are able to find *purpose*—to find out how we can best apply the gifts we possess; how we look at the future. Of course, as black widows, our purpose is weaving a web that becomes our web of life. In addition, meaning is dependent on how we can find pleasure in using our talents—how its use will contribute to a sense of self-efficacy and *competence*. Competence is based not only on knowledge but also on having the imagination and flexibility to deal with the sudden and the unexpected. In addition, it has to do with how we can master whatever we are passionate about; what kinds of activities will give us energy. Look, how we weave and reweave when our webs fall apart! We have practiced over and over again to be able to do so. It turns us into true artisans. Furthermore, meaning has to do with our sense of *control*—the degree to which we believe we are in control of our own destiny. Again, it all has to do with the choices we make; the way we own our own life. For example, just think of how Grandma picks the males in her life. And finally, our search for meaning concerns *transcendence*: the way we manage to connect ourselves to issues that are bigger than us; how we can contribute purposefully to the forest we live in. In other words, it pertains to what each of us can do to make our forest a somewhat better place to hang our webs. Each of us can make a small contribution in that direction. In this context, the meaning of life could be looked at in terms of our guardianship of the world."[2]

---

[2] Manfred F. R. Kets de Vries (2021). *Quo Vadis: Existential Challenges of Leaders.* London: Palgrave Macmillan.

Grandma said: "That was also quite a lecture! I had no idea that we have such a budding philosopher among us. It's very impressive. You gave us much food for thought."

The Great Mother

"Dear little ones, having listened to all of you, it has become clear to me that not too long from now, you will have to weave your own web. And not too long from now, it will be your turn to talk to your own little ones. Your observations about life have made me realize that the clock of time is ticking; that I am getting closer to my expiration date. As you will soon go your own way, it is time to tell you something about our history—not only as black widows but also as members of the female 'tribe.' As one of you already noted, we, as females, represent in a very symbolic way the Great Mother—in other words, Gaia—the primal Mother Earth goddess. As the spiritual embodiment of the earth, she has always been the symbol of fertility, nature, and the flow of abundance. After all, don't we all depend on the earth for food, shelter, and life itself? Therefore, we can look at our female bodies as a sacred metaphor of the earth. And like the earth, all of life is created within these female bodies, whereby bearing little ones can be looked at as a variant of the fertility of the soil. Thus, in a very mystical way, we are held to be one with the earth. Somehow—and again I am pointing out the power of symbolism—the female body is revered as the vessel of creation, transformation, protection, and regeneration."

"Interestingly enough, as black widows, our eight eyes, eight legs, and our body shape in the form of an eight makes us also a symbol of infinity. Just think about it, the sign of infinity is an eight turned on to its side. Therefore, as with another symbolic representation of the Great Mother, we as spiders also represent the cycle of life—its beginning and its end. And what's more, as spiders, we are predestined to be weavers of destiny. We weave the patterns of life. We are busy with construction, destruction, and reconstruction."

"Of course, as has been suggested before—taking more of an in-depth look—the archetype of the Great Mother is simply nothing more than a residue of our relationship with our own mother. Memories of these interactions with times past tend to linger on. And, as all of you have come to realize, this mother image can be formidable. Given the fact that we have the power to give birth, and notwithstanding the fact that males have always tried to dominate us, we are, in reality, the stronger sex."

Attracting and Repelling—A Dangerous Duality

"Of course, it must be clear to all of you that our black widow, Great Mother image, attracts and repels. As I have said before, as females, we symbolize creativity, birth, fertility, sexual union, and nurturing. Without question, we are in possession of a dangerous duality. We possess the power of positive but also negative transformation. In the unconscious, we are not only symbols of the overwhelming power of the forces of nature, embodying sexuality and fertility, but also of a terrifying force—a force of destruction. Naturally, as the Great Mother image, there will always be this shadow self. Therefore, remember—what you suppress or repress will always get expressed!"

"We should accept that the Great Mother Goddess is both the goddess of life but also of death. Actually, the dark twin sister of the Great Mother is the Terrible Mother, this fearful force of destruction. Haven't we all experienced the mother of our childhood as all-giving but also as all-withholding—as good and as bad? And given our very early experiences, this archetype of the feminine inhabits the world of the primordial instincts, frequently represented as a subhuman or even an animal-like form. Thus, as black widows, we also take on a very symbolic role. A prime example of the Terrible Mother archetype—it's terrifying alter ego—is the black-skinned Hindu goddess Kali, a force of death and destruction, a scary apparition with red, raging eyes, disheveled hair, and with fangs protruding from her mouth."

"Furthermore, we black widows are also viewed not only as tricksters but also as witches—these uncanny and unholy representations of the feminine. Again, in taking on this role, we live outside the borders of civilization. Ostracized as we are, we don't necessarily behave according to accepted values. We may not conform; we may not fit into the conventional, more idealized feminine. Instead, we may transgress and cross borders. It explains why we may be called witches. You can imagine, little ones, remembering what I did to your Grandpa, what kind of names his friends are now giving me. As you must realize, most males don't like these untamable aspects that females possess. Thus, once more, attracted as they may be to us, they are also quite scared of us. Perhaps, little ones, I should also add that the dangerous feminine is also closely related to the mythology of the *vagina dentata*—the toothed vagina—whereby a female's vagina is said to contain teeth, leading to male associations of injury, emasculation, and castration. Again, it is no surprise that male spiders are so wary of us. It is no wonder that we face so many hindrances in getting into leadership positions—that we so often face a glass ceiling."

"Thus, to cut a long story short, as females, we are the ones who spin the silken webs—these threads of life and fate—creating webs of endless possibility. We are the weavers of the dreams of destiny, weaving imaginings into reality. The challenge is to make others understand our webs, to have others decipher the red threads that determine destiny. But as the story of your Grandpa showed, many of these others never seem able to manage that. Their puzzlement remains, leaving them all tangled up in the end. It further reinforces the truth of novelist Walter Scott's comment: 'Oh! What a tangled web we weave, when first we practice to deceive!'"[3]

---

[3] Walter Scott, *Marmion: A Tale of Flodden Field*; Canto VI, stanza XVII.

7

When Lions Are Led by a Donkey

After this strange, somewhat surrealistic exposition about male–female relationships, effective leadership and meaning—all seen through the eyes of a spider—I would like to end this book of essays by reminding the reader once more of the disastrous consequences of leader incompetence. Over the years, numerous historians, sociologists, and psychologists have been preoccupied with this theme. To take just one example, in 1961, military historian Alan Clark published his scathing and much acclaimed book *The Donkeys*, in which he examines British generals of the First World War and asserts convincingly that many brave soldiers, the lions, were sent to their death by their incompetent, arrogant, and indifferent leaders, the donkeys.[1] Little could he have known then that his work would resonate so deeply 60 years later.

In the fall of 2020 when reports surfaced that President Donald Trump had expressed disdain for America's war dead, calling them "losers" and "suckers," I could not help but recall Clark's assertions. It made me also think of Norman Dixon's highly unusual work *On the Psychology of Military Incompetence*.[2] In this study, Dixon surveys 100 years of military inefficiency from the Crimean War, through the Boer conflict, to the disastrous campaigns of the First World War and the calamities of the Second World War. What becomes apparent throughout is how authoritarian personalities, whose dysfunctionalities are less noticeable during times of peace, can cause horrible tragedies when war at last strikes.

---

[1] Alan Clark (1961). *The Donkeys.* New York: Morrow.
[2] Norman Dixon (1994). *On the Psychology of Military Incompetence.* New York: Vintage.

When Dixon outlines the psychological characteristics of these military incompetents, it is difficult not to draw parallels with the autocratic, demagogic populist leaders I have portrayed in the various essays of this book. The incompetents that Dixon described are also characterized by a close-mindedness, a lack of intellectual curiosity, and an overall inability to deal with complex situations. What added to their ineffectiveness is that they would distort information in ways to suit their *Weltanschauung*, living under the illusion that they were always right. And their stubbornness was legendary. When things would go wrong, however, they would quickly look for scapegoats. They would also have this irrational belief that mystical forces would come to the rescue when trouble would arise. Furthermore, they weren't strangers to groupthink, which led to feelings of invulnerability and a tendency to ignore adverse information. Furthermore, cultlike behavior was not strange to them.

As Dixon reminded us, subordinates in these military cultures were reluctant to question those in command, making open disagreement a career-endangering move. Sycophancy would rule the way. And against the backdrop of these wildly incompetent leaders, few checks and balances existed to blunt the force or even turn around a disastrous command. Here we should remind ourselves that the impact of military incompetence far exceeds the seriousness of errors in other contexts. Perhaps, the French statesman Georges Clémenceau had a point when he said: "War is far too serious a business to be left to the generals." Of course, the question becomes: are politicians so much better? The essays in this book may have proved otherwise. All too quickly, many of them seemed to become victim of hubris; and all too quickly, like Icarus, they would fly too high!

Leadership When Times Are Tough

However, Dixon's lessons have much to teach any student of leadership. Clearly, many of his warnings are also valid in our day and age. In more ways than one, the pandemic has become another kind of war, given its incredible casualties. But this coronavirus "war" has shown that many of our present leaders didn't have what it takes to deal with this crisis. Their leadership skills were quite absent when faced with the complex circumstances before them. They seemed to have forgotten that leadership is an opportunity to serve, not a demonstration of self-importance.

The renowned businessman Warren Buffett once said: "You only find out who is swimming naked when the tide goes out." Unfortunately, too many of our present leaders have come out quite naked. Anyone can show great leadership abilities when things are easy. The question is how well you will do when everything's falling apart? Thus, what we can see, very much like the generals described by Dixon, is that many suffer from cognitive dissonance, believing themselves to be great leaders, when in fact they have led too many people into disaster. Seduced by the sirens of power, they have managed to claw themselves to the top of the pile, where their incompetence has had dramatic consequences—something very clearly demonstrated in the way many of these leaders have dealt with the pandemic.

In organizations, a poor decision by the top management may have serious financial repercussions that endanger the livelihood of their employees. Those stakes, however, will be far higher in the military where errors can cost hundreds of thousands of lives. The same observation can be made about political leadership. Incompetence, left unchecked, will prove to be catastrophic. Unfortunately, many of our present leaders live in la-la land, appearing somewhat delusional, acting in ways that reflect their contempt for science and other forms of expertise.

Leadership Is a Moral Act

As I suggested before, leadership is a moral act as well as the exercise of authority in ways that go beyond personal interests. Here, as portrayed in the various essays of this book, many of our present leaders' deficiencies stand out in stark relief when compared to the rare people defined by their visionary approach to leadership. For example, after the Second World War, it took a General Marshall to create a plan capable of dealing with the postwar situation. Marshall's personal courtesy and magnanimity, his scrupulous integrity, attention to and command of facts, and broad, humane vision, which resulted in the plan for the post-war European recovery that bears his name, are all a rebuke to many of our present leaders. Many of these populist, demagogic leaders may enjoy some short-term successes, but these are built on a rotting foundation formed out of ignorance and self-centeredness. In the end, they are nothing more than a caricature of the quintessential bad leader: closed to the views of others, humorless except at others' expense, and more interested in perks and deference than in real achievement.

Whether the war being waged is against a global pandemic or an opponent in an armed conflict, it is clear that the cost of having these populist leaders at the helm is staggering. The "Donkeys" should not try to lead the "Lions."

In closing, it is essential to remember that true leadership means tackling tough problems ourselves and not leaving them to our children. It requires the courage to make decisions that will benefit the next generation. We should never forget that real leadership requires that we plant trees under whose shade we will never rest.

Index

A

Absolute power, 17–18
Alternative facts, 12
Anger, 55, 65, 71, 79–81, 88, 103, 110
Angola, 31
Anthony and Cleopatra (Shakespeare), 78
Anti-intellectualism, 53
Anti-social personality, 50
Apple, 111
Arce, Luis, 27
Argentina, 27, 28
al-Assad, Bashar, 27
al-Assad, Hafez, 27
Authenticity, 78, 131
Authoritarianism, 52, 70
Autocracy, 5, 6, 33

B

al-Bashir, Omar, 25
Belarus, 25, 81
Belonging, 11, 134
Bokassa, Jean-Bédel, 18
Bolivia, 27
Bolsonaro, Jair, 77, 78, 80, 81, 84, 85, 87–95, 97–99
Brazil, 28, 78, 93–95
Brexit, 116
Brezhnev, Leonid, 28
Bribes, 24
Buddha, 76
Buffett, Warren, 141

C

Caesar, Julius, Roman Emperor, 18–19
Cambodia, 26
Care, 16, 39, 48, 50, 79, 95, 98, 122, 124, 132–134
Ceaușescu, Nicolae, 18–19
Chávez, Hugo, 26
Childhood, 136
  "spoilt" children, 109
China, 14, 15, 116
Choice, 14, 24, 25, 30, 32, 40, 50, 51, 55, 62, 88, 98, 104, 117, 132–134
Churchill, Winston, 33
Cicero, 116

Clark, Alan, 139
Clémenceau, Georges, 140
Cognitive dissonance, 113, 114, 141
Colombia, 27
Comfort zones, 104, 107, 112
Communication skills, 133
Compassion, 7, 41, 44, 71, 80, 88, 97, 98, 132, 133
Competence, 5, 72, 134
Complexity, 44, 95, 126, 132, 133
Compromise, 105, 106, 111, 112
Confidence, *see* Self-confidence
Confirmation bias, 84
Constitutional amendments, 15, 25
Contempt, 79–80, 92, 141
Control, 5, 11, 17, 29–31, 39, 45, 52, 68, 70, 72, 87, 92, 93, 107, 110, 111, 114, 117, 125, 134
Coronavirus, *see* Covid-19
Corruption, 17, 20, 30, 60, 93, 94
Coups, 18, 25, 26
Courage, 5, 23, 66, 80, 96, 104, 131–133, 142
Covid-19, 6, 70, 71, 73, 95, 140–142
Critical thinking, 12, 84, 132, 133
Crowd psychology, 2, 7–14
Cult-like behavior, 11, 12, 90, 140

D

de Balzac, Honoré, 37
de Kirchner, Cristina Fernández, 28
Dehumanization, 88–89
Democracy, 3, 5, 6, 16, 17, 24, 28, 32–34, 94, 95, 98
Democratic Republic of Congo (DRC), 20
Disinformation, 5
Division, 80, 85, 98
  See also Splitting
Dixon, Norman, 139–141
Donkeys, The (Clark), 139, 142
dos Santos, José Eduardo, 31

Draining the swamp, 92
Duque, Iván, 27
Duterte, Rodrigo, 81

E

Egypt, 26
Elections
  campaigns, 94
  managed, 24–26, 92
el-Sisi, Abdel Fattah, 26
Emotional contagion, 8
Emotional judo, 113, 114
Empathic responsiveness, 95
Empathy, 7, 41, 55, 69, 87, 88, 97, 98, 132, 133
Enablers, 13, 67, 70
Enemies, 3, 30, 59–61, 65, 83, 89, 91, 92
Envy, 23, 81–82, 87, 101
Erdoğan, Recep Tayyip, 14, 31, 81
Evil elite, 3, 6
Extremist belief systems, 90

F

Factoids, 5, 54, 85, 92
Fairy tales, xii, 5, 34–36, 41, 48, 49, 52, 73–76, 78, 92, 93, 99, 103–105, 116
Fan facts, 6, 11, 60
Feminine mystique, xiii, 126–129
Fernández, Alberto, 28
Five pillars of "being", 134
Flattery, 124, 131
Freedom of speech, 4, 5, 85

G

Gaia, *see* Great Mother Goddess
Germany, 1, 19
Governance of China, The (Xi Jinping), 32

Great Mother Goddess, 135, 136
Groupthink
   dynamics, 91
   mentality, 106
Grudges, 95, 107

Hatred
   dehumanization, 87
   hate speech, 85
   intergroup, 86–89
   interpersonal, 86–89
   leading with, 93–95
   learned experience, 88–89
   overcoming, 95–99
   politics of, 90–92
Hesse, Herman, 96
Hitler, Adolf, 1, 2, 6–8, 11–13, 18–19, 83
Hungary, 81
Hun Sen, 26

Idealizing transference, 9
Ideology, 11, 12, 22, 23, 32, 72, 84, 88–90, 116
   creation of, 31
Immigration/immigrants, 3, 38, 60, 95, 102, 103
Income inequality, 3, 4
Inflexibility, 106, 112
Insecurity, 40, 42, 43, 46, 48, 51, 90, 95, 105, 108, 112
Insult politics, 92
Intimacy, 46, 48, 97, 128

Jobs, Steve, 111, 115
Juche ideology, 22, 32

Kabila, Joseph, 20
Kabila, Laurent, 20
Kagame, Paul, 14, 25
Kali, 136
Kim Il-sung, 22
Kim Jong-un, 14, 22–23, 32
Kleptocracies, 29

Leaders for life, 14–34
Leadership
   autocratic, 52, 66, 68
   as a moral act, 141–142
   qualities, 33, 116, 132
   toxic, 14, 99
   values, xii
Lies, 4, 6, 12, 18, 20, 27, 39, 46, 51, 52, 54, 64, 88, 132
Little Red Book (Mao Tse-tung), 32
Love, 46, 52, 76, 79, 80, 86, 93, 95, 126, 127, 134
   love at first sight, 127
Lukashenko, Alexander, 25, 81
Lula da Silva, Luiz Inácio, 28

Machiavellian behaviour, 54, 63, 115, 132
Maduro, Nicolás, 26
Male-female relationships, *see* Relationships
Mao Tse-tung, 32
Marshall, George C., 141
Mass hysteria, 91
Mattner, Walter, 83, 84, 87, 88
Medvedev, Dmitry, 27
Military incompetency, 140
Mimicry, 7–8
Mirror neurons, 8

Mobutu Sese Seko, 19–20
Morales, Evo, 27
Morality, xii, 11, 63
Mubarak, Hosni, 26
Mugabe, Robert, 19–20
Museveni, Yoweri, 20
Myanmar, 26

Napoleon Bonaparte, 18–19, 37
Narcissism, 13, 21, 50, 116
Nazi regime, 1
Nepotism, 29–30
Neuroscience, xii
Nicaragua, 26
Niyazov, Saparmurat, *see* Turkmenbashi
North Korea, 14, 22, 23, 32
Nuremberg, Germany, 1

On the Psychology of Military Incompetence (Dixon), 139
Orban, Viktor, 81
Ortega, Daniel, 26
Ortega y Gasset, José, 4, 85
Outgroup homogeneity, 86

Pandemic, *see* Covid-19
Paranoid thinking, 53–54
Perseverance, 111
Philippines, 81
Political campaigns, 90
Politics of hatred, 90–92
Populism, 3–7
Populist demagogue-like leaders, xi, 2, 5, 93
Post turtles, 16–17, 33
Presidencies
 proxy, 27–28
 term limits, 15
Psychodynamics of power and submission, 107
Psychology
 developmental, xii
 evolutionary, xii
 psychoanalytic, xii
Purpose, 25, 38, 45, 53, 55, 66, 70, 71, 75, 80, 81, 89, 90, 120, 134
Putin, Vladimir, 15, 27, 28, 81

Red herring fallacy, 108
Reflective listening, 113
Relationships, 128, 129, 139
Relationships, male-female
 building, 126
 destructive, 128
 feeling trapped, 129
 power, 131
Religious, 82, 93, 94, 98
Riefenstahl, Leni, 1, 6, 11
Romania, 18, 19
Rousseff, Dilma, 28
Ruhnama (Turkmenbashi), 21, 32
Russia, 27, 28, 81
Rwanda, 14, 25

Santayana, George, 2
Schopenhauer, Arthur, 80
Scott, Walter, 137
Self-confidence, 13, 69, 115, 132, 133
Self-esteem, 6, 37, 113
Self-examination, 5, 89, 97
Selfish herd theory, 7
Self-knowledge, xii
Self-righteousness, 80–81
Separation-individuation matrix, 108–111
Seven Cs, 132–135

Sex, 123–125, 127–129, 135
Shakespeare, William, 78
Sibling rivalry, 82
Social conformity, 9
Social media, 4, 5, 78, 85, 90–95
Social unrest, 4, 29, 33
Soviet Union, 28
Spiders, 116, 117, 120, 122–133, 135, 136, 139
Splitting, 3, 4, 83–86, 95, 98, 105, 112
Stability, 16, 17, 23, 25, 28, 30–33
Stalin, Josef, 6
Stereotyping, 83, 96
Stubbornness
   childhood and, 136
   dealing with, 107, 111–117
Stuckness, 98, 99
Sudan, 25
Swift, Jonathan, 14
Sycophant effect, 12–14

Toxic leaders, 116
Transcendence, 97–99, 134
Triumph of the Will (Riefenstahl), 1, 11
Trump, Donald, 4, 6–8, 11–13, 15, 16, 36, 80, 81, 92, 139
   as "King Drum", 80
Turkey, 14, 31, 81

Turkmenbashi, 21–22, 31
Turkmenistan, 21–22

Uganda, 20
Uribe, Álvaro, 28

Vagina dentata, 136
Venezuela, 26
Victimhood/victimization, 64, 89, 95

Wishful thinking, 93
Women, 38, 45, 53, 54, 78, 83, 94, 123, 124, 126, 128, 129, 136, 137
World War I, 139
World War II, 11, 141

Xenophobia, 2
Xi Jinping, 14, 15, 32

Zimbabwe, 19

GPSR Compliance
The European Union's (EU) General Product Safety Regulation (GPSR) is a set of rules that requires consumer products to be safe and our obligations to ensure this.

If you have any concerns about our products, you can contact us on

ProductSafety@springernature.com

In case Publisher is established outside the EU, the EU authorized representative is:

Springer Nature Customer Service Center GmbH
Europaplatz 3
69115 Heidelberg, Germany

www.ingramcontent.com/pod-product-compliance
Ingram Content Group UK Ltd.
Pitfield, Milton Keynes, MK11 3LW, UK
UKHW021252180426
11946UKWH00004B/100